Best H
CHILDREN

San Francisco's South Bay

Bill McMillon
with Kevin McMillon

THE
MOUNTAINEERS

5
5 4 3 2

Published by The Mountaineers
1011 SW Klickitat Way, Seattle, Washington 98134

Published simultaneously in Canada by Douglas & McIntyre, Ltd., 1615 Venables Street, Vancouver, B.C. V5L 2H1

Published simultaneously in Great Britain by Cordee, 3a DeMontfort Street, Leicester, England, LE1 7HD

Manufactured in the United States of America

Edited by Kris Fulsaas
Maps by Evelyn Phillips
All photographs by Bill McMillon
Cover design by Watson Graphics
Typography by Graphics West
Cover photo: A family enjoys a winter hike through Sunol Wilderness.
Title page: Even toddlers love a walk in the park.

Library of Congress Cataloging in Publication Data
McMillon, Bill, 1942-
Best hikes with children: San Francisco's South Bay / by Bill McMillon with Kevin McMillon.
p.   cm.
Includes index.
ISBN 0-89886-277-9
1. Hiking—California—San Francisco Bay Area—Guidebooks.   2. San Francisco Bay Area (Calif.)—Guidebooks.   3. Outdoor recreation for children—California—San Francisco Bay Area.   I. McMillon, Kevin, 1982-   .   II. Title.
GV199.42.C22S26949   1992
917.94'6—dc20   92-18482
                                                                            CIP

*To Raoul, who introduced me to
many of the joys of hiking*

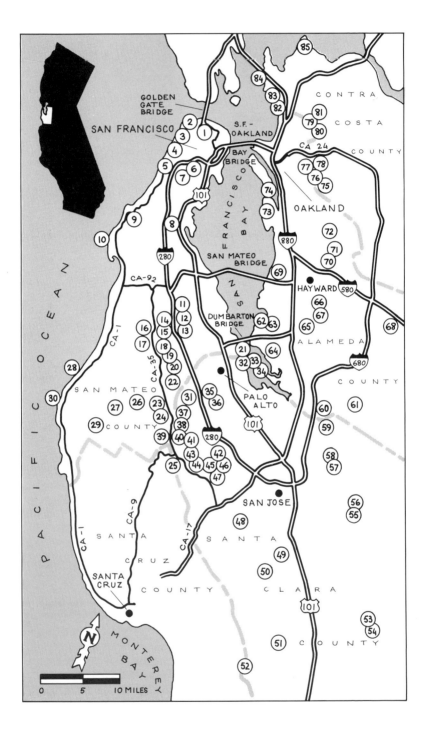

Contents

Let's get going, folks!

Introduction

One of my great pleasures is hiking along a fog-shrouded ridge or through a somber and solemn redwood forest with my wife and my son, Kevin. As a long-time resident of the North Bay, I knew that I had access to a wide variety of such places to hike in the North Bay area.

I had done very little hiking on the San Francisco Peninsula, though, and was not really aware of how many miles of wonderful trails I had missed so close to home. From the top of Skyline Ridge to the deep canyons on the west side of the Santa Cruz Mountains, and around the bay to the oak-covered grasslands of the East Bay Regional parks, there are more than 2,000 miles of trails that lead into vast wilderness areas where few hikers interfere with your enjoyment of nature. Most of these trails were a new experience for me, and I thoroughly enjoyed hiking them as part of the research for this guide.

The residents of the San Francisco Bay Area are truly blessed with so much land that is protected from development, and that is easily accessible to all who wish to use it. Even the cities around the Bay have set aside large parks where families can go for an afternoon hike. There are such large numbers of county and regional parks in the area, however, that very few city parks have been included in this guide. Golden Gate Park, McLaren Park, and many smaller parks along the peninsula have been left out for lack of space, but all are easily reached for those who want to take hikes in an urban environment.

For those who want to head away from the hustle and bustle of city life, the hikes that have been included offer that opportunity. Some are relatively crowded, especially on summer weekends, but many are so lightly used that you may not encounter another hiker on a 5-mile hike through canyons and along open ridges.

From the dense redwood forests of Butano State Park to the open seaside cliffs of Bean Hollow State Park and the high ridges of Henry W. Coe State Park, I have included trails that you can explore with your family, from young children to grandparents. Some are short hikes of 0.5 mile for even the youngest and oldest, while others are more than 5 miles long for those who want to both enjoy nature and engage in pleasurable, vigorous physical activity.

HIKING WITH CHILDREN

Some children can't resist stopping to wade along a slow-moving stream, or watch an acorn woodpecker drill holes in a pine tree. Others want to push on up a trail to reach a hidden beach or an exposed mountain peak as quickly as possible. Each enjoys hikes in his or her own special way, and does so with great bursts of enthusiasm. And parents find such eagerness contagious.

Even the most enthusiastic child sometimes needs a little added encouragement to make it through a day's hike, however, and the following guidelines can help you get through those times—making hikes fun for all.

Know What Your Family Prefers on a Hike

Each family has its own ideas about hiking. While some decide on a destination and concentrate on reaching it, others are more spontaneous, and reaching a particular destination is of only secondary importance. The same is true for members of a family. Some like to surge ahead along the trail to a rest stop where they may dawdle for a while; others like to take a more leisurely pace along the trail with shorter rest stops.

After an outing or two you will know what your family prefers, and you can plan future trips with those preferences in mind.

Plan a Destination

Talk about your destination before you begin hiking, and let everyone know what there is to be seen and explored along the way. Find a creek, a particularly interesting tree, or an outstanding vista, and plan to stop there. You may not make all the planned stops, but your family will have markers to help measure their progress during the hike.

You don't have to be intimately familiar with a trail to do this, for you can find information in this guide, or from other sources, to help plan a hike.

Plan for Nourishment and Rest

Always carry plenty of water, or other liquids, and snacks, even on short hikes. These can be used as incentives when the trail gets steep or the day gets warm, and your charges begin dragging. A simple reminder that "we will stop at the next shady spot to have some water and energy food" gives impetus to continue along the trail.

Also, remember to take plenty of "energy" stops so no one on the hike gets overly tired.

"Adopt" a Child for the Day

You may want to bring a friend or friends along on the hike so each child has a companion with whom to share discoveries and rest stops.

Accentuate the Positive

Praise such as "you certainly did a good job coming up that hill" is important to children, and it lets them know that you are aware of how much effort they are putting into an activity.

If a child shows signs of slowing down on a difficult section of a trail, patience and distractions, i.e., casually observing some trailside plants or rocks as your child overtakes you, or a "look at that soaring hawk," help with progress along a trail.

Tired Children

While most parents have a good idea of how far their children can hike, and plan their outings with those limitations in mind, there are times when the best-laid plans go awry.

There are ways to overcome what are seemingly insurmountable problems, though. In the mid-1970s my wife and I took our four-year-old on a camping trip to Point Reyes National Seashore with a group of high school students. All went well until the last day of the trip, when we discovered that we had neglected to thoroughly study a topographical map of the area. The first portion of the trail from Wildcat Canyon to Bear Valley was a rugged climb, one that no four-year-old could make without help.

Even with the assistance of several teenagers who carried one of our packs and most of our supplies, we began the day with trepidation. The first half-hour went fine, but drastic measures were soon needed. First,

A good talk before starting out lets everyone know what to expect.

Mary and I used our snack supply, and took turns heading up the trail to hide a goody behind a rock or a plant. We then encouraged Matt to scurry up the trail to find them. A successful search was followed by a short energy break while the snack was eaten.

This game got us over the hump, literally, and we made it to our car in a reasonable time. We learned a valuable lesson, however, and ever since we choose hikes that take in the abilities of everyone in the family, checking out the entire trail on a topographic map if we haven't hiked it before.

Of the many ways to avoid such problems on dayhikes, the best is to develop contingency plans for turning back short of your original destination. I have included "turnaround" sites for longer one-way hikes, and the "point-of-no-return" for longer loop hikes where it will be shorter to continue than to go back, to help you with your hike plans.

Have Fun Along the Way

Hikes should be fun. Enjoy yourself and help others enjoy themselves. Explore the area along the trail, and experience the sights, sounds, and smells of nature as you move along the trail. Remember, your goal isn't necessarily to reach a specific destination, but to have an enjoyable outing with your family where your children learn to enjoy and respect their natural environment.

TRAIL ETIQUETTE

Regardless of how well you plan a hike, or how well-behaved your children are, there are times when things don't go right. And there are certain rules of behavior that are expected of all hikers, whether they are children or adults.

The Call of Nature

All the suggestions of "go to the bathroom now, there isn't one on the trail" won't prevent an occasional crisis when your child has to go, and immediately. If the child merely has to urinate, take him or her at least 200 feet from any trail or creek. If your child must defecate, dig a hole at least six inches deep in which to bury the feces. The used toilet paper (and you should always carry a small roll) should be wrapped in a plastic bag, and carried out for disposal.

Uncontrolled Children

Hiking should be fun, but uncontrolled children who run rapidly around blind trail curves, yell loudly, and destroy plants and wildlife aren't fun for anyone. Always set ground rules for your children and any friends brought along on a hike.

Talking about these rules well beforehand lets everyone develop a positive approach toward how to act in the wilderness. Rather than just talking about what not to do, help your children see what others do that is undesirable, and emphasize that "good hikers" don't do those things. By the time you get on the trail, they will be on the lookout for such negative behavior and will need little encouragement to avoid it themselves.

One rule that is frequently violated by children is cutting across switchbacks. Children love to slip and slide down a hill as they run ahead of others, but the practice is devastating to the hillsides, and often leads to washed-out trails. A reminder of the damage caused by this, along with a few examples of damage pointed out on the trail, is usually sufficient.

Family Pets

Don't bring them, even if the rules of the trail say you can. Although Rover may like outings as much as other members of the family, most trails just aren't appropriate for pets, especially if you want to enjoy the plants and animals along the way.

Fires

No fires should ever be built in any of the parks mentioned here except in designated sites at campgrounds and picnic areas. This is extremely important, because most of the trails in this guide are in and near habitats that become extremely volatile during the hot, dry months between May and October. Many parks even have rules against smoking on their trails during dry summer months.

Trail Right-of-Way

While hikers have as much right to the use of the trails in this guide as any other group, simple courtesy and a sense of safety say that hikers should give the right-of-way to mountain bikers and horseback riders. When you hear them coming, step off the trail, wait for them to pass, and avoid any loud noises or sudden movement as they do.

Leave Nothing but Footprints; Take Nothing but Photos

The hikes in this guide are in regional, state, or national parks, all of which have rules about collecting or destroying plants, animals, and other natural items. Help your children understand these rules, and why they exist. If you are unsure of what the rules are for any park where you plan to hike, contact the local rangers for information, which they are always glad to furnish.

This is an opportunity to develop a wilderness ethic for your family by emphasizing how parks have been set aside for all to enjoy, and that destruction of plants and animals (and collecting often has the same results as heedless destruction), as well as unsightly littering, defeats that purpose.

ENJOYING NATURE

While hiking can be an end unto itself, most children like to investigate the ins and outs of the world around them, and that includes sites along trails. A creek becomes something more than just a body of water to be crossed. It becomes a place to investigate: a place where smooth, round rocks can be skipped across large pools; where insect larvae can be discovered under slimy bottom rocks; where frogs can be found in creekside vegetation; and where feet can be soaked as energy food is consumed.

The same is true of trees, boulders, and hillsides. All provide many attractions to your children, and you can utilize this interest to introduce the study of nature, and you can do so in a sharing way.

Sharing, Not Teaching

Let your children share in your interests as you walk along the trail and at rest stops. Point out a wildflower that you like. If your child is interested, discuss where the flower grows, what insects are around it, and other particulars that you can observe—and you can do all of these without ever knowing the flower's name.

You don't have to teach the children anything. They can experience it right along with you. And you can experience anew the delight of investigating a creekbed, a tree, or a bluff through their eyes.

Use All Your Senses on the Trail

Watch the light fall across a meadow, smell a pine tree, and touch a thistle. Even taste a limestone rock. All these will give you and your children a variety of sensations with which to experience nature.

Getting the Feel of Nature

When your child complains about the trail being hot and dusty, ask how the animals in the area cope with the midday heat, and where they get their refreshments. Suggest that the shade of the forest ahead may bring about a change in mood, and offer a drink or snack to help refresh the body as well as the spirit. Once you reach the shady forest, discuss how the animals that live nearby might enjoy similar breaks during their day.

Relating moods and experiences to the wildlife that lives in the region helps you and your children become more in touch with the natural world, and adds immeasurably to your hiking experiences.

With these suggestions, and thoughts of your own, you should be able to find trails in this guide that will give you many hours of pleasant outdoor activity. Go, and enjoy, but first be sure to make some pre-hike preparations.

GETTING READY FOR DAYHIKES

While it is possible to simply get in your car and drive to a hiking trail with no preparation, it is not necessarily wise. A little preparation makes all hikes more enjoyable, and may prevent unnecessary trouble.

The Ten Essentials

The Mountaineers recommends ten items that should be taken on every hike, whether a day trip or an overnight. When children are involved, and you are particularly intent on making the trip as trouble-free as possible, these "Ten Essentials" may avert disaster.

1. **Extra clothing.** It may rain, the temperature may drop, or wading may be too tempting to pass up. Be sure to include rain gear, extra shoes and socks (especially a pair of shoes that can be used for wading), a warm sweater, and a hat and light gloves.

2. **Extra food.** Extra high-energy snacks are essential for active children and adults. Carry sufficient water in canteens and fanny packs in case no suitable source is available on the trail.

3. **Sunglasses.** Look for a pair that screens UV rays.

4. **Knife.** Chances are you will never need it, but bring one along anyway. A knife with multiple blades, scissors, a bottle opener, and tweezers is a must.

5. **Firestarter—candle or chemical fuel.** If you must build a fire, these are indispensable.

6. **First-aid kit.** Don't forget to include moleskin for blisters, baking soda to apply to stings, extra sunscreen, and any special medication your child might need if he or she is allergic to bee stings or other insect bites.

7. **Matches in a waterproof container.** You can buy these matches in a store that carries hiking and camping gear.

8. **Flashlight.** Check the batteries before you begin your hike.

9. **Map.** Don't assume you'll just "feel" your way to the summit. Maps are important, and I discuss them more later in this introduction.

10. **Compass.** Teach your children how to use it, too.

In addition to these ten essentials, the following suggestions will help make hikes more enjoyable.

What to Wear

There is little need for special clothes or shoes for dayhiking in the San Francisco Bay Area. Trails are generally well marked and stable. They don't demand heavy-duty hiking boots, and specialty clothing is rarely called for since we have such an equable climate.

Active-wear shoes such as those your children wear to school and for playing around home are perfectly adequate. Sneakers, especially high tops, give all the support needed, and have the advantage of being well-broken in. This helps keep blisters to a minimum, thereby avoiding one of the most uncomfortable aspects of hiking.

To enjoy hiking in the San Francisco Bay Area, it is important to wear enough of the right kinds of clothing to keep you comfortable in changing weather. This means layers that can be removed and put back on as the day's weather changes from windy and foggy to sunny and warm—and back again. Because hiking is a year-round activity in the Bay Area, and there are so many microclimates throughout the region, it is difficult to say exactly what clothing you should carry on any one hike. The only thing certain is that you are likely to need layers of clothes any time of year, on any hike.

Rain gear is generally important only in the winter, with an occasional storm in the fall or spring, but a hat or a cap is useful year-round to protect adults and youth alike from the effects of the sun.

Packs

Not everyone has to have a pack on a dayhike, but children love to carry their own to hold their special items. Adults' day packs should be large enough to carry bulky clothing and extra food and drinks, but youngsters can use either day or fanny packs. The only requirement is that the packs should be large enough for some food, small items such as magnifying glasses, individual drinking containers, and layers of clothing that have been removed.

Other Items

Other items you may want to bring along to help make hikes more fun include light-weight binoculars (one pair per family should do, but some families have several) for looking at birds and animals, as well as scouting the trail ahead; a magnifying glass and insect boxes for short-term viewing of small animals and plants; a light-weight camera for recording the trip; and possibly some nature guides to help identify objects in the field as they are observed. You can use your knife to dig around in old stumps and under rocks when searching for creepy crawlers.

None of these items is essential for the enjoyment of hikes, but all help you and your family explore the world of nature closeup, and provide activities that can be pursued during rest breaks and eating times.

Maps

Since these trails are in developed parks, you are unlikely to get lost on any of these hikes, although some of the longer ones do take you away from the most heavily traveled areas of the larger parks. However, a little common sense, a copy of the park brochure, and an awareness of where the trail is should keep you on track.

Topographic maps with contour lines and marked trails aren't strictly necessary, but can be fun and interesting for children. When combined with an inexpensive compass they can be used to determine your exact

Parks have something for all ages, from moms to babies in strollers.

position on the trail, as well as provide a new and interesting learning experience.

Topographical maps of the region and compasses, as well as instruction books on how to use them, are sold in most hiking and camping stores in the Bay Area.

Food and Drinks

Outings are a good time to let your children have high-energy foods such as candy bars and other sweet snacks as treats. These can be used as motivation to get to that shady tree up the trail where you can stop for a rest, or over the hump to the top of a ridge. You can also take along other foods such as fruit and high-protein foods that the children like for lunch breaks.

Children like to carry some food in their own packs, but you can hold back special treats until they are needed for motivation.

Remember also that one of the "Ten Essentials" is extra food. Whatever you take on the hike, don't skimp. It is always better to carry extra food home than to have hikers become cranky and disagreeable from hunger.

Another item that you absolutely must not skimp on is fluids. Many of the hikes in this guide can be hot and dry during the summer months, and few have drinking water available.

While sugary and sports drinks are fine for replacing lost fluids, never depend solely upon them. On Kevin's sixth birthday we took a group of boys on a hike to Lake Ilsanjo in Annadel State Park, and took along only snack drinks to have with lunch and along the trail. The June day was hot, there was no potable water at the lake, and several of the group complained loudly about their need for "real" water during the 5-mile round trip to the lake and back.

First Aid and Safety

First aid and safety are generally big items in hiking books, but in reality I have found that my children have less need for first aid on the trail than during a normal day.

Nevertheless, my "Ten Essentials" first-aid kit includes large and small Band Aids, antibacterial cream, a squeeze bottle of hydrogen peroxide, a patch of moleskin, some scissors, an athletic bandage, a medicine for relief of insect stings, and some itch medicine. Recently I have also begun carrying a cold wrap, but I must admit this is more for me than for my children.

Though not technically first aid, sunscreen and insect repellent should also be carried. While biting insects aren't a major problem in the Bay Area, there are times when mosquitoes and flies can be bothersome, and the repellent helps. Sunscreen is an absolute necessity, especially for those of us so fair-skinned as to "burn while on the backside of the moon," because many trails cover long distances where there is little or no shade.

In addition to the normal scrapes and falls that accompany active children, nature also offers several things that are, if not dangers, at least worries that parents must be aware of and caution children about.

Poison Oak, Nettles, and Thistles. These are all plants that can precipitate either an immediate or a delayed reaction that causes discomfort, and you should be aware of what these plants look like during various seasons.

Stinging nettles cause a more immediate reaction than poison oak (which generally doesn't appear for two days to two weeks from exposure) and can be quite painful—even excruciatingly so—to children and adults alike. Various types of thistles also cause intense pain and itching for some people.

Itch medicines help with, but don't completely relieve, the discomfort of stinging nettles. The best solution is to avoid contact. If you don't know what the various plants look like, park rangers will be glad to help you identify them, and many parks have signs illustrating poison oak and nettles. If you are hiking in areas such as Point Reyes, where nettles and thistles are abundant, you may want to take along a guidebook with which to make a positive identification.

Stinging Insects. Some parks in this guide have large numbers of stinging insects such as yellow jackets, and these can be scary to children. While their stings are painful, they don't have to be cause for ending a hike. Over-the-counter medicines are available that relieve the discomfort when rubbed on a sting.

Rattlesnakes. Rattlesnakes are another thing that parents fear, and many parks in this guide have large populations of rattlers that come out during warm spring and hot summer months. Very few hikers ever see these reclusive animals, though, and a few simple precautions are all that are necessary to avoid a bite: Never stick your hand down into rocky crevices without first looking. Never climb rock faces where you have to put your hands into holes for handholds. Always watch where you are stepping when you step over logs and rocks.

Rattlesnakes are poisonous, and they do occasionally bite people, but their bites are seldom fatal. If, by chance, a member of your hiking party is bitten by a rattlesnake, don't panic. Have the person who was bitten lie down and remain still, and send another member of the group to find a ranger or a phone. Let the authorities, whether a ranger or 911, know where the victim is located, and when the bite occurred. With modern medicine, there is little danger if medical attention is given promptly.

Lost and Injured Children. I have tried to emphasize the reality of danger on trails in the Bay Area, but most are minimal. Two dangers, however, stand out above all others, and adults can do much to control them. The first is injury and death from falls around cliffs. Children love to climb on rocks and cliffs, and have great fun doing so, but the crumbly sandstone cliffs that are so common along the Bay Area shoreline are the most dangerous that can be found. No one, children or adults, should climb on them because they present definite and immediate danger. Even walking too close to the edge of these cliffs places hikers in danger.

The second danger is of children straying from the group and becoming lost and panic-stricken. Search-and-rescue units spend many hours searching for lost children in the parks of the region, and members often speak to school and youth groups about how to avoid this lonely and terrifying experience. First, they advise that everyone carry a loud whistle. Second, they recommend that anyone separated from the group, and unable to gain attention with a whistle, "hug" a tree (or a bush or boulder). This means the child should sit down next to a tree, or bush, or boulder, and stay there until found. The only other action the lost person should take is to blow a whistle or shout loudly at regular intervals.

With these simple precautions and preparations, you should find that hiking the trails of the San Francisco Bay region will be a satisfying way to spend family outings.

NATURAL HISTORY OF THE SAN FRANCISCO BAY AREA

A wide variety of plant and animal communities, including some such as the coast redwood forests that are only found in Northern California, are found around the San Francisco Bay. Many hikers enjoy their outings without ever learning anything of significance about either the plants or the animals that they may encounter on the trail, but I find that I enjoy my outings a little more when I learn something about the various natural communities, and how the plants and animals interact with each other. For those who want to learn more about the various plant and animal communities of the San Francisco Bay region, both the University of California Press and Wilderness Press publish a number of natural history guidebooks that are very useful. The following are a few examples of the flora and fauna that you are likely to see in your wanderings.

Chaparral

Many hills of California are covered by a dense growth of hard-leafed, drought-resistant plants collectively known as chaparral. The plants in this community are well adapted to the long, dry summers and wet winters of Northern California, for they tolerate the hot dry spells and protect the hillsides during the wet winter months. In addition, they regenerate very quickly from fires.

The plants in these communities include various species of manzanita, which has shiny red bark on its trunk and branches and ranges from low creepers to 15-foot-tall shrubs; ceanothus, sometimes called California lilac, with its large clusters of blue or white flowers; and chamise, a member of the rose family that spreads into almost impenetrable thickets that are 2 to 10 feet high.

Coastal Scrub

The plants in these communities are softer than those in chaparral, and the dominant plant is coyote brush. Coastal scrub is found near the ocean and bay, where there is more moisture and less heat.

Wildflowers

Wildflowers such as California poppy and blue lupine are familiar to everyone who has driven along the highways of Northern California, but there are dozens more native wildflowers that can be identified along the trails in this guide.

Trees

Several species of trees are so common in the region that you will probably encounter at least one species on almost every hike in this book. These include the many species of oak that are native to the region (and it is hard for some people to distinguish between these); various species of exotic eucalyptus (which were brought here from Australia in the nineteenth century); bay, which is also known as California laurel, pepperwood, and myrtle; buckeye, a member of the horse-chestnut family; madrone, with its distinctive smooth red trunk and peeling bark; Douglas fir, an important lumber tree that grows to a height of 300 feet; and the coast redwood, the tallest tree in the world.

Mammals

Raccoon, opossum, gray squirrels, chipmunks, ground squirrels, rabbits, coyote, gray fox, bobcat, and black-tailed deer are some of the more common animals that you are likely to either encounter or observe signs of along the trails of San Francisco Bay Area parks. In some parks you may even see signs of bear and cougar, but you're not likely to run into either.

None of these present any danger to hikers, with the possible exception of bear and cougar (and there have been no reports of attacks by either in the Bay Area in many years), and children are delighted to see animals in their natural habitat.

Sea lions and harbor seals are often spotted in and around the bay and ocean.

Birds

Various hawks, vultures, jays, and a number of types of gulls are all common in the region, and a bird guide will help you identify the many smaller birds that you will run across on your hikes.

HOW TO USE THIS GUIDE

The hikes in this guide are located in the Bay Area counties of San Francisco, San Mateo, Santa Clara, and Alameda, and are located within county, regional, state, and federal parks and reserves. Most parks provide maps or brochures that describe the trails within their boundaries, and tell something about the natural history of the region. You can obtain these either at the parks or from park district offices. Addresses and phone numbers of park districts are listed at the end of this introduction.

Although the trails in the guide are permanent, there is always the possibility that one will be closed because of landslide, fire danger, or other natural condition. In addition, park officials sometimes reroute trails or close them temporarily for other reasons.

You can call the park where you intend to hike to ask about the latest trail conditions and find out if the trail you intend to use is open. If it isn't, you can ask about similar trails nearby and most park officials will gladly help.

While the number of hikes in this guide may seem like a lot for the region, they represent a small percentage of the total miles of trails that are available in the four counties. The East Bay Regional Parks have 1,000 miles of trails, and it is only one of several large park systems in the region.

The hikes that are included were selected with several thoughts in mind. One was that there be some hikes that anyone, even those barely past the toddler stage and those who are quite elderly, could enjoy. Another was that the majority be moderate hikes from which most families would derive a sense of accomplishment after completing, and the last was that some be difficult enough to challenge older children (up to twelve years old) in good physical condition who like to hike.

The hikes also cover the wide range of natural habitats that exist in the Bay Area. Open grasslands, oak woodlands, mixed oak and madrone forests, mixed conifer forests, redwood and fir forests, tidelands, and seashore are all represented, and you will see a wide variety of flora and fauna as you walk along the trails.

Entries for the hikes include information about length, difficulty, and location, and tell something about the natural history of the region covered by the trails.

One last thought. This is a guide to dayhikes in the Bay Area, but several of the park systems in the region have developed environmental and hike-in campsites where you can backpack in for one or more nights. These are not covered here, but you may want to investigate the possibilities after you have explored many of the trails, and want a more adventurous family outing.

PARK DISTRICT HEADQUARTERS

The following is a listing of the district headquarters of the local, county, regional, state, and national parks where the hikes in this guide are located. If you have any questions about the conditions of the trails— whether it is too wet or hot or dry to hike in the park, what wildflowers are blooming, etc.—give them a call. They are always willing to answer questions, or refer you to someone who can.

California State Parks
PO Box 9
Pescadero, CA 94060
408-879-0173

East Bay Regional Park District
11500 Skyline Boulevard
Oakland, CA 94619
510-531-9300

Golden Gate National
  Recreation Area
Fort Mason, Building 201
San Francisco, CA 94123
415-556-0560

Henry W. Coe State Park
PO Box 846
Morgan Hill, CA 95038
408-779-2728

Midpeninsula Regional
  Open Space District
Old Mill Office Center
Building C, Suite 135
201 San Antonio Circle
Mountain View, CA 94040
415-949-5500

San Francisco Bay National
  Wildlife Refuge
1 Marshland Road
Fremont, CA 94536
510-792-0222

San Mateo County Parks
  and Recreation
590 Hamilton Street
Redwood City, CA 94063
415-363-4020

Santa Clara County Parks
  and Recreation Department
298 Garden Hill Drive
Los Gatos, CA 95030
408-358-3741

Although not part of the park system, there are several trail and hiking organizations in the Bay Area that have current information on trails and hikes. These include:

Trail Center
4898 El Camino Real
Office 205 A
Los Altos, CA 94022
415-968-7065

Santa Cruz Mountains
  Trail Association
PO Box 1141
Los Altos, CA 94023
415-948-9098

A NOTE ABOUT SAFETY

Safety is an important concern in all outdoor activities. No guidebook can alert you to every hazard or anticipate the limitations of every reader. Therefore, the descriptions of roads, trails, routes, and natural features in this book are not representations that a particular place or excursion will be safe for your party. When you follow any of the routes described in this book, you assume responsibility for your own safety. Under normal conditions, such excursions require the usual attention to traffic, road and trail conditions, weather, terrain, the capabilities of your party, and other factors. Keeping informed on current conditions and exercising common sense are the keys to a safe, enjoyable outing.

THE MOUNTAINEERS

KEY TO SYMBOLS

 Dayhikes. These are hikes that can be completed in a single day. While some trips allow camping, only a few require it.

 Easy trails. These are relatively short, smooth, gentle trails suitable for small children and first-time hikers.

 Moderate trails. Most of these are 2 to 4 miles in total distance and feature more than 500 feet elevation gain. The trail may be rough and uneven. Hikers should wear lug-soled boots and be sure to carry the Ten Essentials.

 Difficult trails. These are often rough, with considerable elevation gain or distance to travel. They are suitable for older or experienced children. Lug-soled boots and the Ten Essentials are standard equipment.

 Hikable. The best times of year to hike each trail are indicated by the following symbols: flower—spring; sun—summer; leaf—fall; snowflake—winter.

 Driving directions. These paragraphs tell you how to get to the trailheads.

 Turnarounds. These are places, mostly along moderate trails, where families can cut their hikes short yet still have a satisfying outing. Turnarounds usually offer picnic opportunities, views, or special attractions.

 Cautions. These mark potential hazards—cliffs, stream or highway crossing, and the like—where close supervision of children is strongly recommended.

 Environmental close-ups. These highlight special environmental elements along the trail and help children learn about and respect nature.

ACKNOWLEDGMENTS

Although I did all the writing for this guide, my nine-year-old son Kevin is listed as coauthor, and for a very good reason. Without his interest in hiking and nature, it may very well have never been written. As a companion on the trail, and as a constant push at home (especially when he attempted to compute what his share of the income from the book would be), Kevin has played an important role from start to finish.

My wife, Mary, also deserves mention, for she has been a trail companion for more than twenty years, even though she prefers what she describes as "Midwest walks" where there are few hills, which sometimes conflicts with my desire to reach the highest spot around. Her suggestions on what to include in the trail entries were taken seriously.

Finally, I wish to thank the people at The Mountaineers Books for giving me the opportunity to share some of my favorite hikes with others.

LEGEND

═══	MAJOR ROAD
▬▬▬	SECONDARY ROAD, PAVED
═══	UNPAVED ROAD
=====	FIRE ROAD, JEEP TRAIL (NO MOTOR VEHICLES)
••••••	HIKING ROUTE / TRAIL
•▬•▬•	PAVED TRAIL
----	OTHER TRAIL
Ⓣ	TRAILHEAD
Ⓟ	PARKING
→	DIRECTION OF HIKE
⚠	CAMPGROUND
☗	PICNIC SITE
⚊	GATE
) (	FOOTBRIDGE
～～	RIVER OR STREAM
⳩	MARSH
△	VIEWPOINT OR PEAK
⊏⊐	BENCH
+++++	RAILROAD RIGHT OF WAY

San Francisco and San Mateo Counties

Coastal walks lead through many different plant communities.

1. Presidio Ecology Trail Loop

Type: Dayhike
Difficulty: Moderate for children
Distance: 2-mile loop
Hiking time: 2 hours
Elevation gain: 200 feet
Hikable: Year-round
Map: Golden Gate National Recreation Area Park Guide

The Presidio has been staffed by soldiers since the first Spanish garrison arrived there in 1776, making it the oldest continuously used military post in the United States. The Presidio Army Museum, located at the corner of Lincoln Boulevard and Funston Street, documents the 200-plus years of military occupation of this beautiful corner of San Francisco. Early soldiers at the Presidio complained of the harsh envi-

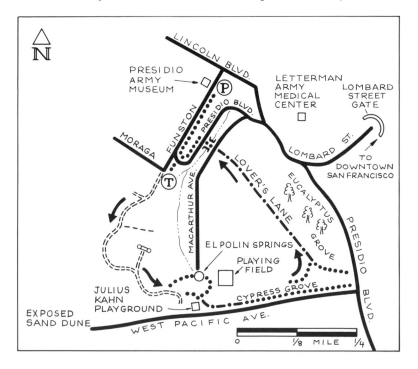

ronment of the sand dunes where the fort was located and the Army Corps of Engineers developed a plan to landscape the area with non-native trees in 1883. More than 60,000 trees were planted in the area during the 1880s alone, and today's visitors can see at least 30 different types of trees along the Ecology Trail Loop and many more, including acacia, cypress, eucalyptus, madrone, redwood, spruce, and Portuguese cork oak, can be seen throughout the Presidio.

Enter the Presidio at the Lombard Street Gate, and curve around the Letterman Army Medical Center on Lombard until it dead ends at Lincoln Boulevard. Take a left on Lincoln and go one block to Funston. Turn left on Funston and left again into the parking lot across the street from the museum.

To reach the trailhead for the Ecology Trail Loop, head southwest along Funston Street for about 0.25 mile, where Funston dead ends. The trail begins straight ahead as a fire road.

The trail winds along the side of a hill and goes through a forest of eucalyptus, Monterey pine, and other exotic trees that were planted to help retain the sand dunes and break the monotony of the barren land that the Presidio was built on. Have your children count how many different kinds of trees and shrubs they can distinguish, and discuss why the Presidio planted them.

At about 0.5 mile from the parking area a trail heads off to the right, but veer to the left and continue around the hillside. After another 200 yards a narrow trail leads downhill to the left. Continue straight ahead on the fire road.

A grassy meadow opens up on the hillside above the trail at about 0.75 mile, and the views of the forest below from the meadows makes them a pleasant place to take a rest.

Several hundred yards past the hillside meadows the trail dead ends into another fire road. Take a right.

Housing is visible downhill from the trail as it veers to the right around the hill. At about 1 mile a small park can be seen downhill on the left, and a small, lightly used trail leads down to it. You may take the trail down to the park for a rest at the picnic site near the historic site of El Polin Springs. The springs were the primary source of water for the early Spanish soldiers at the Presidio, and were used for many years. You can talk about the history of the Presidio as you take a break, or you can head up the steps to the south of the picnic site to the Julius Kahn Playground, where there are slides and other play equipment.

You can also reach the playground by continuing along the main trail. It passes through a section of exposed sand dunes just a few hundred feet before the playground, and then becomes a paved walkway.

The walkway continues past the playground beside West Pacific Avenue and leads through a cypress grove. At about 1.25 miles an easily missed trail leads off to the left. This trail takes you to the paved Lover's

Creekbanks are a delight to explore.

Lane, but if you miss it and end up at Presidio Boulevard, simply turn left for about 100 feet along Presidio until you come to the signs for Lover's Lane.

Take a left there, and head downhill to MacArthur Avenue. A large eucalyptus grove is uphill from the lane and a housing unit is downhill.

Lover's Lane crosses MacArthur Avenue at about 1.75 miles. A small meadow between MacArthur and Presidio is divided by a creek. Cross the meadow, the small brick footbridge, and Presidio Boulevard before turning left.

Continue up Presidio for about 100 yards until you reach Funston. Turn right on Funston, and return to the parking lot.

You may want to make a visit to the museum where the children can learn about the history of the Presidio.

2. Fort Point–Baker Beach Coast Trail

Type: Dayhike
Difficulty: Moderate to difficult for children
Distance: 4 miles round trip
Hiking time: 3 hours
Elevation gain: 300 feet gain and loss
Hikable: Year-round
Map: Golden Gate National Recreation Area Park Guide

The 2-mile stretch of oceanfront cliffs and beach between Fort Point beneath the Golden Gate Bridge and Baker Beach has a long military history. From the Gold Rush period before the Civil War until World War II, Fort Point and a number of bunkers and gun batteries were built to protect San Francisco harbor from invasion by enemy forces. These fortifications were never used in war, and slowly became obsolete as military strategy changed with the advent of nuclear weapons and ICBMs. The relics of these earlier eras remain for adults and children to explore, however, and serve as good rest stops on this hike between Fort Point and Baker Beach.

Follow the signs from the south of the toll plaza of the Golden Gate Bridge to the parking lot for Fort Point at the end of Marine Drive. The

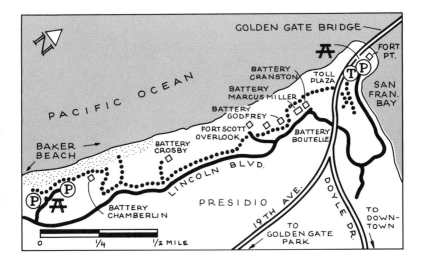

trail leads uphill toward the southern end of the bridge from the picnic area at Fort Point.

The trail ascends from Fort Point with a series of switchbacks along the bay side of the bridge. This continues for several hundred yards to a junction where one trail leads to an observation platform near the toll plaza, one to the left toward several bunkers, and one to the right under the bridge. Take the trail to the right and head along the top of the cliffs. From here you can look back north to the Marin Headlands or south toward Lands End.

The trail leads along the edge of the cliffs and at about 0.5 mile Battery Cranston and Battery Marcus Miller can be seen to your left. You can explore these cleverly camouflaged fortifications now, or wait until you return. Your children will love to explore as many of these batteries as you let them, and sometimes they will get distracted from the hike. Emphasize that there are a number of batteries along the trail, and that you will be returning on the same route.

The trail heads inland as you pass these batteries, and at about 0.75 mile comes to a parking lot adjacent to Merchant Drive. Battery Boutelle is located here, and is more accessible than the first two were.

A bare-footed walk on the beach, a beautiful view of the Golden Gate Bridge, and solitude can all be found at Baker Beach.

A few hundred feet past Battery Boutelle the trail passes by Battery Godfrey, and comes to a small side road that leads to the Fort Scott Overlook. This overlook is a good rest stop.

From the Fort Scott Overlook the trail again turns inland and is soon separated from Lincoln Boulevard by only a barrier. There is poison oak alongside the trail on this section, and occasional heavy traffic, so caution your children of the dangers.

At just past 1 mile a side trail leads down to Battery Crosby. This side trip is about 0.25 mile each way.

At about 1.25 miles another side trail leads down to Baker Beach over sand dunes. This area is being re-vegetated, and you should stay on the trail and not explore on the dunes. You can head down to the beach here, or continue on the main trail to Battery Chamberlin at 1.5 miles. There are plans for this battery to be reconstructed so that visitors can see how the fortifications operated, but the lack of funds may delay the opening.

The trail reaches Baker Beach at 1.75 miles, and continues to the end at 2 miles. Baker Beach has parking and picnic sites toward the southern end, and more than 1 mile of beach extending northward toward the Golden Gate.

Return to Fort Point along the same trail. One adult may stay with the children while the other returns to Fort Point if the return hike seems too difficult, or two cars can be used, one at each parking lot.

3. Coastal Trail to Lands End

Type:	Dayhike
Difficulty:	Moderate for children
Distance:	1-mile loop
Hiking time:	2 hours
Elevation gain:	200 feet loss and gain
Hikable:	Year-round
Map:	Golden Gate National Recreation Area Park Guide

Lands End is the wildest, rockiest part of the coastline around San Francisco. The cliffs are unstable, and landslides frequently crash down during heavy storms. The area immediately off the point is just as dangerous, for many ships have run aground on the submerged rocks there.

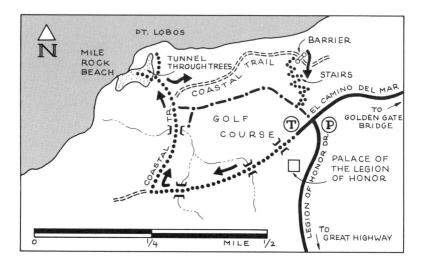

Wildflowers are profuse here in the spring.

Park in the parking lot of the Palace of the Legion of Honor at the corner of El Camino Del Mar and Legion of Honor Drive. From the lot walk to El Camino Del Mar and turn left. The trailhead is about 200 yards ahead, at the end of El Camino Del Mar.

The trail almost immediately crosses a small footbridge and begins a gentle swing around the top of a small canyon. The large creek in the canyon is fed by several small springs and creeks that the trail crosses.

Just before 0.5 mile the trail veers to the right as a fire road continues straight ahead. Take the trail to the right as it begins to head downhill in a series of steps. As it levels off at about 0.5 mile it dead ends into the Coastal Trail. Turn right on the Coastal Trail, cross the large creek, and join another fire road about 100 yards past the creek.

A right turn here takes you uphill to the golf course and the paved golf cart trail. Turn left, and go for about 50 yards on the fire road to a trail that leads off to the left. This trail heads down to Lands End, and passes through a ghostly forest of dead cypress trees. When fog shrouds the cliffs, the stark, gray crags can fill a child's imagination with many wonderful and scary images.

At about 0.75 mile, just before the trail dead ends at Point Lobos, another trail leads off toward Mile Rock Beach. You must travel through about 50 feet of tunnel formed by coastal scrub and cypress before you reach the top of the beach. The tunnel and beach are a good play area and rest stop that the children will enjoy.

As you return to the trail to Point Lobos, take the short trail out to the end, and on a clear day the view is spectacular. On foggy days the sound of the surf far below adds to the eerie feeling of loneliness that often accompanies walks along the cliffs.

Return to the Coastal Trail, turn left, and continue to a barrier that blocks any further progress at about 0.9 mile. At that point a narrow trail leads up the side of the cliff back toward the golf course. About halfway up the steep wooden steps there is a bench that offers a good view of the coastline on clear days.

Continue up the trail until it dead ends at the paved golf cart trail. Turn left to return to the parking lot.

Fog shrouds a ghost forest near Lands End.

4. Sunset Trail–Fort Funston

Type: Dayhike
Difficulty: Easy for children
Distance: 0.75-mile loop
Hiking time: 45 minutes
Elevation gain: None
Hikable: Year-round
Map: Golden Gate National Recreation
Area Park Guide

Fort Funston, with its great dunes, sandy bluffs, and steady ocean breezes, is one of the premier hang-gliding areas in the San Francisco Bay region. Wildflowers bloom profusely on the dunes and along the trails during the spring and early summer, and children love to explore Battery Davis, a casemated battery that was completed in 1938. It was the prototype for all sixteen-inch gun emplacements built in the United States after that.

Drive south on the Great Highway until it becomes Skyline Boulevard at Lake Merced. Turn into the Fort Funston parking area about 0.5 mile past John Muir Drive, and continue to the rear of the parking area near the viewing deck.

Take the short walk to the viewing deck where your children will like to observe the hang-gliding area, and get a good view of Burton

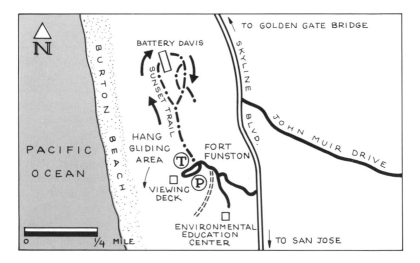

Bunkers and gun emplacements from pre–World War II are slowly being overgrown at Fort Funston.

Beach below. Return to the parking lot, and head north on the Sunset Trail. This was the first wheelchair-accessible trail to be built along the California coast, and it is an easy trail for the whole family, even those with babies in strollers, or grandparents in wheelchairs.

Benches and picnic tables are scattered along the side of the trail as it leads through open dunes and coastal scrub until it reaches Battery Davis at just under 0.5 mile. Children like to explore this old fortification, and you may want to discuss why they were built, and the mood of the country during the 1930s.

The paved trail leads through the battery, encircles it, and returns to the parking lot at 0.75 mile.

Beware that this is one of the few trails around San Francisco that allows dogs to run free. Because of this it is often overrun with dogs that at least seem to be out of control. If you have small children, or older ones who are afraid of large dogs, let them know that there will be dogs on the trail. You also must watch for piles of dog poop along the path.

5. Sweeney Ridge Trail to San Francisco Bay Discovery Site

Type: Dayhike
Difficulty: Difficult for children
Distance: 4 miles round trip or loop with return via Sneath Lane
Hiking time: 3 hours
Elevation gain: 500 feet plus loss and gain of 300 feet in ravine
Hikable: Year-round
Map: Golden Gate National Recreation Area Park Guide

More than 200 years ago Gaspar de Portola became the first European to view San Francisco Bay as he and his men reached the 1,200-foot-high summit of Sweeney Ridge in November 1769. Today this windswept ridge is little different—still covered with coastal scrub and grassland—from what it was when Portola first explored the area. Since then it has served as a military outpost, most recently as a Nike missile site during the 1950s, and as a part of the Golden Gate National Recreation Area.

 Hikes along Sweeney Ridge and close-by Milagra Ridge offer outstanding views of the Pacific Ocean, San Francisco Bay, and the mountain ranges of central San Mateo County. There are four endangered species in the Sweeney Ridge area: three butterflies—Bay Checkerspot, Mission Blue, and San Bruno Elfin—and one snake, San Francisco Garter. You may wish to look these up in a field guide before you take your hike so that you can identify them.

 Turn on College Drive off Skyline Boulevard south of San Francisco to Skyline College. As you enter the campus turn left, and park in the first parking lot on the left. This is parking lot No. 2 and is open to visitors. From the parking lot take a right on the paved service road behind the lot and walk uphill past the maintenance barns.

The first 0.75 mile of the trail winds around the edge of a low hill on a fire road. This area is open, with occasional patches of coastal scrub. Have the children keep a watch out for small animals and birds along here, and look up to see if any raptors (birds of prey such as hawks and eagles) are soaring overhead.

At about 0.75 mile you come upon an old building that is in disrepair. This is a good place to rest and look out over the San Francisco Bay to the east. Have the children try to guess what the building was used for (a guardhouse for the Nike missile site), and why it may have been necessary. Also have them compare the region as it was when Portola and his men first reached Sweeney Ridge and as it is now.

As you leave the guardhouse the trail divides and heads downhill. The trail drops 300 feet here and immediately gains it back on the other side of the ravine. You can take either branch, for they both lead to the creek at the bottom of this steep hillside. The trail is not well constructed here, and little has been done to build switchbacks that hold back erosion. Caution your children about sliding down the hill, and explain that switchbacks should be here to help avoid erosion and make it easier to descend the hill.

At the bottom of the hill you will cross a seasonal creek and begin an equally steep ascent up the other side. Again the trail forks, and both lead to the same spot up the hill. I prefer the left fork for it takes you by a seepage area with small springs and vegetation that is a little thicker. If you are quiet, or are out in the early morning or evening, you may see small mammals such as raccoons and foxes around the springs. Birds are always flitting around in the trees and shrubs.

The trails rejoin at the lower reaches of the ridge, and at about 1 mile the Sweeney Ridge Trail joins with the Mori Ridge Trail, which comes in from the right. Turn to your left on the wider fire road. This takes you along a slight incline through heavier coastal scrub where there are plenty of birds and profuse blooms of wildflowers in the spring and early summer.

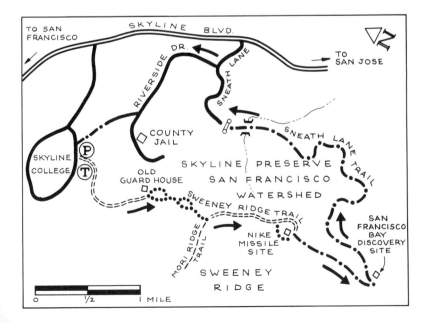

Sweeny Ridge offers excellent views of San Francisco Bay.

The fire road circles around the radar station of the old Nike missile site at just under 1.5 miles. As you approach the site a small spur trail leads off to the right, but you have easier access to the site as you round the curve just past the spur.

The fire road becomes paved at the old site, and for the next 0.5 mile or so is an easy hike on level paved road. At 2 miles you come to the San Francisco Bay Discovery Site. At this level, open site there is a stone plaque honoring Portola's expedition, and a granite monument nearby that depicts views that can be seen from this high spot on clear days. These include the Farallon Islands to the northwest, Mount Tamalpais and the Point Reyes Peninsula to the north, Mount Diablo to the northeast, and the Montara Mountains and San Pedro Point to the south.

You can return to the parking lot by the same route, or you can head downhill on the paved Sneath Lane Trail. This trail takes you about 1.25 miles to Sneath Lane, which you follow for another 0.25 mile to Riverside Drive. Take a left on Riverside, and continue for a little over 0.25 mile. Just before you enter the parking area for the county jail, take a right and follow the road for about 0.25 mile back to parking lot No. 2.

6. Saddle/Bog Trails Loop

Type: Dayhike
Difficulty: Moderate for children
Distance: 2.5-mile loop
Hiking time: 2 hours
Elevation gain: 150 feet
Hikable: Year-round
Map: San Mateo County Park

San Bruno Mountain stands as an open-space island in the midst of a densely populated urban area, and offers excellent hiking opportunities with outstanding views of San Francisco, the East Bay, and the San Francisco Peninsula to the south. Popular support of local conservationists helped block development on the mountain and get the area established as a state and county park to protect fourteen species of rare or endangered plants and two species of endangered butterflies. The mountain, which rises to 1,314 feet at the top, may be covered by fog any time of the year, and winds can be quite strong there. The slopes are brightly colored with wildflowers in the spring and early summer, and there is plenty of birdlife in the region. Even small mammals seem to be making a comeback here, and you can often see signs of raccoon, fox, coyote, and bobcat as you hike the trails.

Take Guadalupe Canyon Parkway west from US 101 to the exit to the park. Follow the signs, and park in the lot to the north of the parkway. The Saddle Trail leads out to the right from the rear of the picnic area.

The first portion of the trail winds through light coastal scrub as it loops around the contour of the hill. The slopes along this section are covered with profuse blooms of wildflowers in the spring and early summer. The trail levels out at about 0.5 mile, but continues around the contour of the hill. As it turns around the contour there is an excellent view of the bay and the East Bay hills. Mount Diablo is straight ahead.

At just before 0.7 mile there is a bench where you can sit and look out over the bay, the Oakland/San Francisco Bay Bridge, and downtown San Francisco.

As the trail continues around the hill it passes through a grove of eucalyptus and Monterey pine, with San Francisco still visible on the right. At the 1-mile trail marker you can take a short spur of about 100 feet out to an overlook. The view is excellent here.

The trail begins to head uphill past the overlook. There are springs all along the hillsides here. Ask the children how you know there are

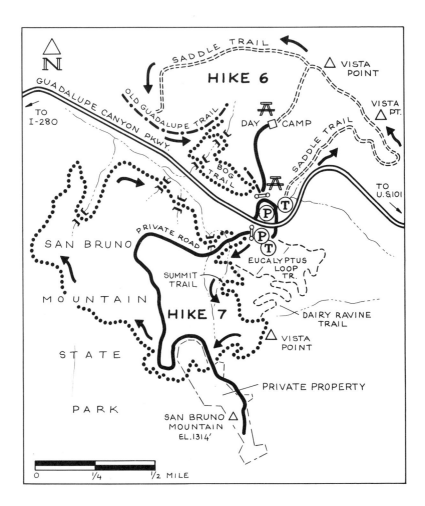

 springs (the lush, green growth that is very different from the surrounding plants).

At 1.25 miles a trail leads off to the left. This leads down to a day camp where there are picnic tables and water. This is a good stop if the camp is not in session, and is a return route back to the parking lot if your young ones are getting tired.

The trail again heads uphill from here and you soon have fine views of Twin Peaks and the Marin Headlands, with Mount Tamalpais standing high above all.

From 1.25 to 1.5 miles the trail is a roller coaster, and at 1.5 miles you come to a saddle where you begin to head downhill. At about 1.75 miles the trail follows around a chain link fence and comes to a large

eucalyptus grove. Have the children try to find some seed pods and smell
some of the leaves.

The Saddle Trail dead ends at the Old Guadalupe Trail at just before 2 miles. Take a left on the paved trail as it leads through groves of eucalyptus, willows, and brambles. There are some acacia and cypress at just past 2 miles.

The Bog Trail leads off to the right just past 2 miles. Wild strawberries grow alongside the trail. At 2.25 miles there is a bench where you can sit and look out over the bog. About 100 yards past the bench the trail splits. Either branch takes you back to the parking lot, but the trail to the right is a little wilder. Take this if your children would like to explore more, or take the left and pass over a wooden footbridge.

The trail passes uphill from the bog and through a grove of cypress and there are plenty of ferns on both sides of the trail. Have the children look at the different types of fronds on the fern.

The trail that veered to the right and went around the wild side of the bog rejoins the trail from the left at about 2.4 miles, and the Bog Trail comes back to the Old Guadalupe Trail just before you reach the parking lot.

Wildflowers of all types are found throughout the spring and summer on South Bay hikes.

7. Summit Trail Loop

Type: Dayhike
Difficulty: Difficult for children
Distance: 3-mile loop
Hiking time: 3 hours
Elevation gain: 725 feet
Hikable: Year-round
Map: San Mateo County Park

Although the previous hike was a gentle introduction to San Bruno Mountain State and County Park, the Summit Trail Loop is a rugged, long hike that takes you up the steep north slope to the summit of San Bruno

Walking the trails on San Bruno Mountain can be a lonely experience.

Mountain, and then follows a long, gradual return down the ridge to Cable Ravine. The trails offer outstanding vistas of San Francisco, the East Bay, the Peninsula, and the ocean; there is plenty of birdlife to keep everyone alert during most of the year; and the hike along the ridge after you reach the summit leads through large areas of blooming wildflowers during the spring and early summer. Many of the wildflowers here are rare and cannot be seen anywhere else. It is well worth the time to obtain one of the fine wildflower guides on the park before you take a spring hike. This is a strenuous hike, and probably should not be attempted with children under eight years of age.

Follow directions to hike 6, but do not enter the parking lot to the north of the parkway. Instead, continue on the road as it circles back under the parkway to the parking lot on the south side. The Summit Trail leads out of the west end of the parking lot.

The trail heads into a grove of eucalyptus. The first portion of the trail leads through this grove, which is almost an enchanted forest with ivy vines growing up over stumps and snags of old eucalyptus forming various spooky shapes. Have your children talk about what the covered logs and stumps look like to them.

At the first junction at 0.1 mile take the trail to the left and leave the grove of eucalyptus. The trail begins a series of sharp switchbacks through a heavy cover of coastal scrub. In about 100 yards there is another junction. Take the right and stay on the Summit Trail. The section of trail from about 0.2 mile to 0.6 mile continues up steep switchbacks through a fragile environment. Please keep on the trail here, and observe from a distance the many wildflowers that bloom here in the spring and early summer.

At 0.6 mile the Dairy Ravine Trail leads off to the left. About 100 feet past this junction there is a short spur on the left that leads to a vista point with a bench. This is a good place to take a break as you take in the panoramic view of the bay and the East Bay hills. Although you have not reached the summit at this point, you have come close. If the young hikers in your group are getting tired this is a good turnaround point. You can return to the junction of the Dairy Ravine Trail and head back downhill to the Eucalyptus Trail Loop for a hike of just over 1 mile.

If you wish to complete the Summit Trail Loop, head uphill from the vista point. There is a trail leading off to the left as you reach the private property just before 1 mile. There are a number of satellite antennae, transmitter towers, etc. along the ridge. You don't get to the 1,314-foot summit as you cross the ridge since it is on private property.

After crossing the private property you begin a long descent downhill toward Guadalupe Canyon Parkway. The descent is about twice as long as the ascent, and the slope is much less. Between 1 and 1.5 miles there is scattered coastal scrub. At 1.5 miles there is a bench that looks straight toward downtown San Francisco and the San Francisco/Oakland Bay Bridge.

There is a lone Monterey pine located at about 1.5 miles. Ask the children how they think the pine got there. Is it a native or exotic? (There is an old roadbed that heads off uphill about where the tree is.)

There is some sign of bobcat, coyote, and deer along this section of open trail, but there is not much sign of wildlife for such an open area.

As you reach about 2 miles there is plenty of wind year-round on the open ridge. This impedes the growth of any high plants since the wind dries the plants.

At about 2.25 miles the trail crosses a year-round creek with plenty of riparian growth of willow and alder.

At 2.5 miles you have reached the bottom of the trail as it reaches the lush riparian growth. A spur leads straight ahead to the creek from the trail. This spur trail leads to the banks of the large creek that parallels Guadalupe Canyon Parkway, and this is a good place to take a break and let the children explore for signs of small animals and birds.

The spur trail takes a sharp turn and heads upstream back to the main trail at 2.5 miles, and the rest of the hike is at a slight grade uphill. There are a number of feeder creeks that come from springs on the hillside. Small footbridges cross several of these. Look for birds on both sides of the trail along this section.

At 2.9 miles you re-enter the eucalyptus grove as you cross a small creek that should have a nice waterfall just above the trail after winter rains. The trail crosses a paved service road as it enters the eucalyptus grove, and you can either turn left on it to return to the parking lot or continue straight on the trail to the lot.

8. Quail Trail Loop

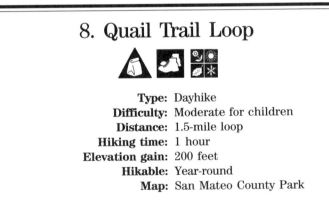

Type: Dayhike
Difficulty: Moderate for children
Distance: 1.5-mile loop
Hiking time: 1 hour
Elevation gain: 200 feet
Hikable: Year-round
Map: San Mateo County Park

The 100 acres of Junipero Serra County Park are noted for the abundance of spring wildflowers, both on the open grass-covered hillsides and in the wooded areas on the north slopes. The park is nestled into a small triangle between I-280 and the city of San Bruno. Native trees

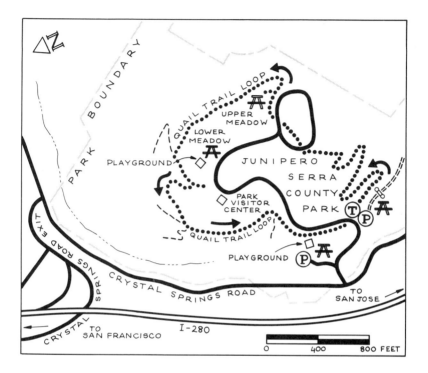

found in the park include several species of oak, California bay, buckeye, willow, and madrone. Exotics include several species of eucalyptus, Monterey cypress, and Monterey pine. Poison oak is very abundant throughout the park and should be avoided.

Take the Crystal Springs exit off I-280 at San Bruno, and turn right on Crystal Springs Road. Continue for just over 0.5 mile to the park entrance. Turn right after the toll booth and park in the Willow Shelter parking lot. The trailhead is on the east side of the parking lot at the flagpole.

Live oak and poison oak cover the hills on both sides of the trails here. Wild iris are plentiful in the early spring, and native bunch grass can be seen.

Above the oak at 0.2 mile there are Monterey pine. This is about the northern extreme of their natural range.

Above them, at about 0.3 mile, there are a number of different species of eucalyptus. Have the children look at the different types of leaves, seed pods, and shape of the crowns and trunks. Even the bark is different. Have them find some different leaves. Crush them and see if they have different smells as well.

As you pass the eucalyptus, a group of pine towers above a layer of pine needles. Discuss the formation of duff, and the volatility of dry pine

Some of the best views of San Francisco can be enjoyed from the north slope of San Bruno Mountain.

 needles, eucalyptus leaves, and chaparral. Also discuss the lack of undergrowth beneath the pine.

The trail continues uphill and passes some eucalyptus trees with multiple stems that have grown since they were either cut or frozen back.

The trail crosses a paved road at 0.5 mile, and then heads over the ridge where you overlook the San Francisco Airport and Mount Diablo in the distance.

At just past 0.6 mile a trail leads off to a picnic area. The trail continues around the contour of the hill and at about 0.75 mile there is a grassy meadow above the trail with a children's play area. This is a good place to stop for a break, since the children can play on the equipment while the adults eat, take a break, and look out over the bay.

There is a grove of redwood trees downhill from the meadow.

Just before 1 mile a broad trail leads off to the left to the visitor center, and the Quail Trail Loop veers to the right. There is a large patch of poison oak alongside the trail here.

Another fork is located just past 1 mile. The right trail leads down to a city park. Take the left on the Quail Trail Loop. This section of the trail leads through some chaparral and a spring flows out of the hill above the trail.

At about 1.2 miles take a left at the fork where the nature trail leads off to the right. There are a number of very climbable oak along here, but beware of the poison oak.

There are also a lot of low-lying brambles alongside the trail here.

At 1.4 miles the trail comes out beside the paved road above a play area with a picnic area, climbing equipment, and volleyball courts.

As the trail returns to the parking lot you pass the trailhead for the Live Oak Nature Trail. This 1-mile-long, self-guided loop is shorter and has less climbing than the Quail Trail Loop, for those with very young children.

9. Brooks Falls Overlook Trail/Old Trout Farm Trails Loop

Type: Dayhike
Difficulty: Moderate for children
Distance: 1.5-mile loop
Hiking time: 1 hour
Elevation gain: 150 feet
Hikable: Year-round
Map: San Mateo County Park

San Pedro Valley County Park, 1,150 acres, has two freshwater creeks that flow year-round through lush valleys. These are the south and middle forks of San Pedro Creek, and both are significant because they provide some of the rare spawning areas for migratory steelhead in San Mateo County. The spawning season is generally between December and February. During this time, and until the end of the rainy season, the 175-foot-high, three-tiered Brooks Falls is a special attraction along the south fork of the creek. Many sensitive plants live in the streamside habitat provided in the park, with several different trilliums, many fern species, creek dogwood, and arroyo willow all found along the creekbanks. The

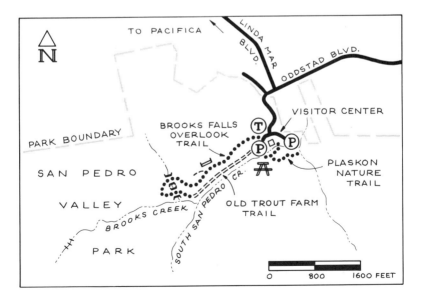

slopes and meadows offer a colorful array of wildflowers in the spring. Wildlife is abundant in the park, with many birds and small mammals. The short (0.03-mile) Plaskon Nature Trail is a good introduction to the plant life of the park, and should be taken before beginning the longer Brooks Falls Overlook Trail/Old Trout Farm Trail Loop.

Take Linda Mar Boulevard off CA-1 in Pacifica, and continue until it dead ends at Oddstad Boulevard. Take a right turn on Oddstad, and the entrance to the park is about 50 yards on the left. Park in the lot to the right of the visitor center. The Plaskon Nature Trail is behind the visitor center, and the Brooks Falls Overlook Trail begins behind the rest rooms at the rear of the parking lot.

Before starting your hike, you may wish to take a walk to the rear of the visitor center where the short, self-guided Plaskon Nature Trail introduces you to the various plants found in the park.

After taking the nature trail you can head uphill on the Brooks Falls Overlook Trail. For the first 0.25 mile the trail leads along the contour of the hill through a mixed forest with several exotics such as eucalyptus and Monterey pine. There is heavy undergrowth here, including thick stands of poison oak.

After about 0.25 mile the trail begins a steeper climb up the hillside through a thick stand of eucalyptus. Although there are some old, large trees in this grove, there are also many very young ones. Talk to the children about how the eucalyptus reproduce very rapidly when the conditions are right, and obviously there were several years in the past decade where those conditions were excellent, for these stands of young trees are very defined.

At about 0.5 mile there is a bench on the uphill side of the trail that overlooks the deep canyon of Brooks Creek, and to the right offers an excellent view of the three-tiered Brooks Falls (or it does when the falls are active). Immediately past the bench there is a trail that leads off to the right. Do not take that trail, but head downhill to the left.

The trail leads downhill, where it crosses a feeder creek and levels out as it follows the contour of the hill on the opposite side of the creek. The trail leads into an area that was obviously once a homestead. There are steps, concrete retaining walls, and some paths that are left of what was a large home. Just below the home, after you have descended down some stone steps, you will find the remains of a garden and some old garden ponds.

At about 0.75 mile the trail winds around to follow Brooks Creek until it joins South San Pedro Creek. Although there are several spots along the creek where children can explore, including one where a fallen tree spans the creek, caution them that this is a spawning creek for migratory steelhead, and that their spawning grounds should not be disturbed.

Brooks Creek joins South San Pedro Creek at about 1 mile, and the

Open trails often lead into dark forests in South Bay parks.

trail becomes Old Trout Farm Trail as you turn left. This section of the trail is a wide road that once led to a trout farm in the area, and follows along the creek. Again, there are several access points, but caution the children to only look and not disturb the steelhead.

The trail returns to the parking lot and picnic area at 1.5 miles.

10. James V. Fitzgerald Marine Reserve Trail Loop

Type: Dayhike
Difficulty: Moderate for children
Distance: 1-mile loop
Hiking time: 1 hour
Elevation gain: 50 feet
Hikable: Year-round
Map: San Mateo County Park

The reefs and marine life have been studied in James V. Fitzgerald Marine Reserve for more than seventy years, and twenty-five species of invertebrates and plants that were new to science have been discovered

Coastal walks offer fantastic views of the coastline from high cliffs.

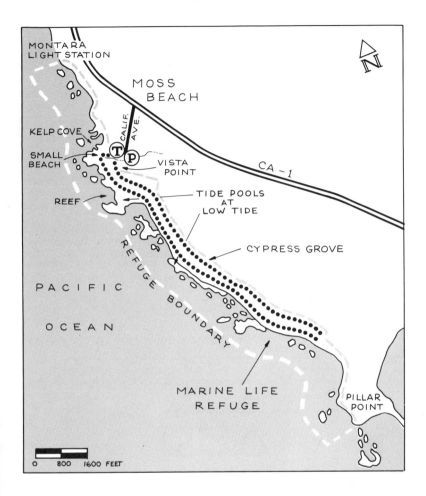

here. In addition, there are several endemic species (ones that live no-
where else) found here. The reserve was set aside in 1969 to protect the
fragile and complex marine communities so that we and future generations can enjoy them. The reefs offer excellent tide pools for exploration,
especially during low tides. All marine life is protected within the reserve
except for some game fish, so do not collect specimens.

Follow the signs in Moss Beach (CA-1 to California Avenue) to the
reserve parking lot

From the parking lot head down the paved trail toward the beach,
but take the trail to the left over the wooden footbridge. After about 100
feet the trail takes you to a lookout point where a wooden fence keeps
hikers from getting too close to the edge of the sandstone cliffs.

From the vista point follow the trail south along the fence and through a cypress grove. At 0.5 mile the trail begins to descend to the beach. If the tide is too high to follow the bottom of the cliffs along the reefs, you must retrace your route after a stop on the beach at the south end of the reserve.

If the tide is low you can take a walk along the bottom of the cliffs, explore the many tide pools, and climb over the rocks. The best tide pools are obviously at very low tide, but there are some worth exploring any time the reefs are exposed at all. On the day I was there, and it was not a particularly low tide, a great blue heron stood in one of the pools for the entire time hunting for fish and small marine invertebrates.

Have the children search around the tide pools to see if they can find any starfish, sea anemones, hermit crabs, or other small marine animals that live in this tidal zone. When they spot a sea anemone have them gently place their fingers in the center of the anemone to see how it closes up to capture prey. Starfish may be gently lifted from the water so that the children can feel their rough surfaces and see the suction cups on the bottom of their tentacles.

You return to a more open beach at about 0.75 mile. You can take a break and play there, or you can hike past it to Kelp Cove where you may see some seals and various water birds.

11. Pulgas Ridge Open Space Preserve Trail Loop

Type: Dayhike
Difficulty: Moderate for children
Distance: 3-mile loop
Hiking time: 2 hours
Elevation gain: 400 feet
Hikable: Year-round
Map: Midpeninsula Regional Open Space District

Cordilleras Creek originates in the canyons of this open space preserve, and a broad, high meadow sits between two wooded canyons. During the spring this is one of the premier wildflower sites on the peninsula. The 293 acres in the preserve lie just north of Edgewood County Park, and feature many of the same animal and bird habitats and plant communities.

Take the Edgewood Road exit off I-280 and head east for 1 mile. Turn left on Crestview Drive and take another left immediately on Edmonds Road. Park at a roadside turnout after the first curve on Edmonds.

From the turnout take a right through the gate and walk just over 0.5 mile on a paved easement road through a valley owned by the San Francisco Water District. As you reach the gate to the preserve, the road turns left and then heads uphill to the high meadow where a tuberculosis hospital once stood.

The meadow is now encircled by an oak forest and is filled with brilliant wildflowers in the spring. It is a good spot to have a picnic on warm spring or fall days.

From the meadow the paved road continues to the top of the preserve at just over 1 mile, where there are views of canyons on both sides of the ridges. During the spring wildflower bloom, this is an impressive site.

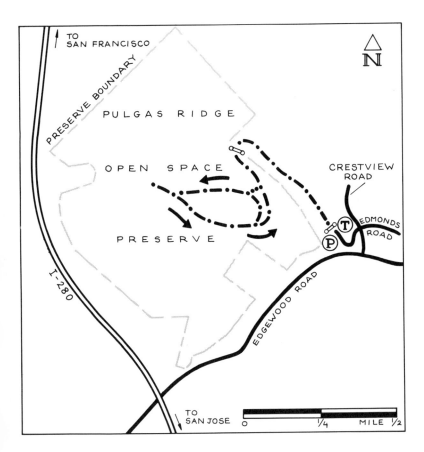

During the long blooming season here have the children keep track of the many different species of flowers that they locate along the trail. Help them spot small, low-lying flowers that they might miss without bending low and searching diligently.

Remember, you don't have to know the names of the flowers to enjoy their beauty. In fact, children love to give their own names to flowers, and later compare them with those given in field guides.

Walk to the end of the paved road near the water tank and return, following the road around the other side of the meadow to the parking area.

By the time this guide is completed, there should be an alternate trail in the preserve that leads off the paved road about 200 feet before the entrance gate and climbs through the tree-covered canyon in the northeastern section of the preserve. This trail will join the paved road near the water tank, and you can then proceed to the meadow. This will be a 3.5-mile loop.

A solitary jogger enjoys a peninsula trail that is free of hikers.

12. Edgewood/Ridgeview/Sylvan Trails Loop

Type: Dayhike
Difficulty: Difficult for children
Distance: 5-mile loop
Hiking time: 3 hours
Elevation gain: 600 feet
Hikable: Year-round
Map: San Mateo County Park

The open grasslands in Edgewood County Park sit on serpentine hills and are famous for their spring wildflower displays. In addition, the 467 acres in the park feature oak woodlands and chaparral plant communities that are home to many small mammals and dozens of species of birds. Seven rare or endangered plant species have been identified in the park. These include the San Francisco thornmint, which was thought to be extinct for a number of years. The bay checkerspot butterfly, which once was plentiful around the entire Bay Area, is now found only in this park and two others—Jasper Ridge and San Bruno Mountain.

Take the Edgewood Road exit off I-280 and head east for 1 mile to the entrance of the park. Turn right at the Edgewood Park and Day Camp sign, and cross the bridge to the parking lot. The trailhead is on the west side of the lot.

Edgewood Trail begins a steep uphill climb out of the parking lot and leads through a mixed forest with buckeye, oak, and madrone. A thick undergrowth of toyon and poison oak covers the ground on both sides of the trail.

A service road crosses the trail just past 0.25 mile. Edgewood levels out somewhat along this section, and the uphill slope is a grass-covered meadow that is filled with brilliant wildflowers during the spring.

The trail continues to climb slowly through a shaded oak/madrone forest, and at about 0.5 mile the Sylvan Trail leads off to the left. If you feel that the young ones in your party won't be able to make the full 5 miles of this hike, this is a good turnaround. A left on Sylvan back to the parking lot makes about a 1.75-mile loop along wood-shaded trails.

For those who wish to make the entire loop, continue straight. The trail hugs the steep contours of the canyons that drain the northwest side of the park, and the steep canyons are blanketed with a thick cover of bay trees.

At about 1 mile the trail leaves the shade of the forests and enters

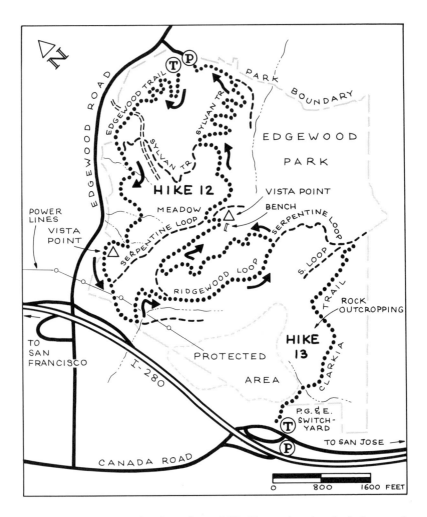

an area of open grassland on the uphill side, and a stand of chaparral on the downhill side. A spur trail leads off to the right for about 100 feet at about 1 mile, and there is a small knoll with large rocks that makes a good picnic and rest stop. The views from here are good, and the wildflowers are spectacular in the spring.

CAUTION   The children may wish to explore around the rocks for lizards, but let them know that there are rattlesnakes in the park. They should not stick their hands into any crevices where they do not have a good view, and they should be careful before sitting on any rocks.

After the rest stop the trail heads downhill, passes another service road that crosses the grassland, and goes under a power line.

At just under 2 miles Edgewood Trail ends. Serpentine Loop continues straight ahead and crosses a creek area with good stands of willow, and the Ridgeview Loop is to the left as it heads uphill into a wooded area.

You may wish to continue to the creek area, where there are large numbers of birds, especially during the nesting season, and backtrack to Ridgeview before heading uphill. Children like to explore along the edge of this marshy area.

Ridgeview Loop leads up a small canyon through grassland, and then turns uphill toward an oak forest. After about 200 yards there is a fork, with a trail leading off to the left. If your party is getting tired, you can take this trail to cut about 1 mile off the loop. It leads around the north slope of the ridge, while the other leads around the south.

Take the right fork to complete the loop. The trail leads through a forest of large trees, and out into an open hillside by 2.5 miles. Uphill is a stand of chaparral, and to the right is a fantastic view of open grass meadows that are dotted with multiple hues of wildflowers in the spring.

At about 2.75 miles the trail comes to a junction. Straight ahead takes you to the Serpentine Loop. Take the left to head along the top of the ridge through a heavy growth of chaparral. Have the children discuss why the shrubs of the chaparral are so much smaller than the oak and bay of the rest of the park.

Fallen leaves carpet trails during the winter and fall.

After several hundred yards of chaparral, the trail again enters an oak forest and begins to descend.

At about 3 miles Ridgeview Loop dead ends. Take a right on Sylvan Trail, and continue downhill. In this stretch you have a view over the meadow that the Serpentine Loop traverses, and there is a bench where you can stop and enjoy the view at about 3.25 miles.

There is a trail junction at about 3.5 miles where the Sylvan Trail crosses the Serpentine Loop. Continue straight ahead on the Sylvan Trail as you cross the open grassland, and head for another canopy of oak and buckeye.

Just before 4 miles the trail splits. The trail to the left leads back to the Edgewood Trail, and the one to the right is the Sylvan Trail that leads back to the parking lot. Take the right fork, which goes downhill. The next mile leads you through a thick forest that offers shade from the hot afternoon sun, which makes the other trails somewhat uncomfortable on warm days.

13. Clarkia Trail

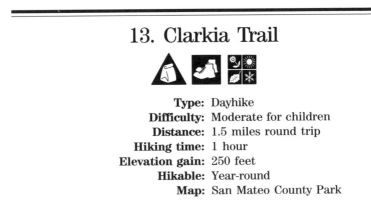

Type: Dayhike
Difficulty: Moderate for children
Distance: 1.5 miles round trip
Hiking time: 1 hour
Elevation gain: 250 feet
Hikable: Year-round
Map: San Mateo County Park

In contrast to the variety in the plant communities found along the Edgewood/Ridgeview/Sylvan Trails Loop, the flora along the Clarkia Trail on the west side of Edgewood Park is limited. This doesn't make it an uninteresting trail, though, for it passes along one side of a protected area that includes many of the rare and endangered plants found in the park. After it passes the protected area, it continues around the contour of an exposed hillside with rock outcroppings and extensive chaparral growth. On sunny winter days, this is an excellent hike because of its southern exposure.

 Take the Edgewood Road exit off I-280, and head west for about 0.5 mile to Canada Road. Turn left and continue back under I-280. Park in the pullout across Canada Road from the P.G.&E. switchyard. The trailhead

Small, colorful wildflowers can often be spotted by those who watch the ground near trails.

is across Canada Road from the pullout.

As you go through the gate into the park, there is a sign indicating that the open hillside to the north of the trail is a protected area. A number of the rare or endangered flowers and plants that grow here are very fragile. Remind your children of the need to preserve rare plants, and make sure they stay on the trail.

During late winter and early spring the wildflowers here present an especially brilliant display of blooms. The protected area actually only adjoins the trail for several hundred yards, but hikers should stay on the trail for good distances on both sides to ensure that no rare plants are harmed.

Several large streams flow down from the hillsides just past 0.25 mile. The plant growth around the streams is significantly different from that just short distances away. Ask the children why they think this is so.

Just before 0.5 mile there is a large rock outcropping that juts out over the trail. Children like to climb around the edges of this, but make sure they know about rattlesnakes and don't put their hands into places they can't see clearly. Downhill from the rock outcropping the hill descends steeply down to a creek far below. Warn any children who might try to climb down that this is a dangerous area.

The trail leaves the open grassland and enters a thick cover of chaparral several hundred yards past the rocks. This section of the trail can be extremely hot and dry in the summer, but is a pleasant hike during a winter afternoon as it is warmed by the southern sun.

The trail dead ends at 0.75 miles, and you return to the trailhead by the same route.

14. Chickadee Trail

Type: Dayhike
Difficulty: Easy for children
Distance: 1-mile loop
Hiking time: 1 hour
Elevation gain: Minimal
Hikable: Year-round
Map: San Mateo County Park

Huddart County Park's 973 acres include several different plant communities. In the deep canyons, and along streams and gullies, large second-growth redwoods provide a cool, shaded environment for ferns and sorrel. On the top of the ridges the cool shade gives way to a hot, dry environment where chaparral shrubs such as manzanita, chamise, and chaparral pea form thick, almost impenetrable brush. In between stands mixed evergreen forests with tanbark oak, madrone, bay, and fir. Each of these communities is home to a variety of mammals and birds. The Chickadee Trail is an almost level, wheelchair-accessible trail that leads through examples of each of the above plant communities.

Take the Woodside exit off I-280, and head west on Woodside Road for about 2 miles. Turn right on Kings Mountain Road and go about 1.5

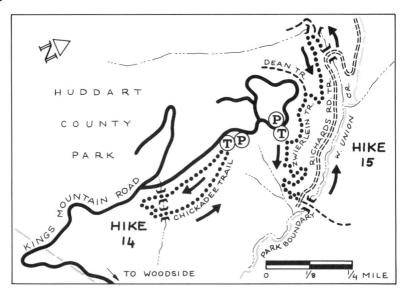

miles to the park entrance. Park in the first parking lot on the right and the Chickadee Trail leads out of the rear of the parking lot.

This is a well-marked trail with cables on each side. Take the right at the fork. After about 0.1 mile the trail leads into a redwood grove and crosses over a wooden footbridge. There is a grove of young redwoods uphill of the smooth, easy trail, and a view across the bay on the downhill side.

There are toyon and madrone downhill just before 0.25 mile. Have the children feel the smooth, hard, dense wood of the madrone that is beside the trail.

Just past the madrone there is an oak grove, with some moss-covered boulders uphill. Talk to the children about how moss and lichen help break down large boulders into rock and gravel, which is in turn broken down into soil.

About 100 yards past the boulders there is a bench. Below is a small circle of redwoods that have grown from an old stump. You can discuss with the children that this is one way that redwoods regenerate, by sprouting up from the roots of old redwoods that have died or been logged. The circles they can observe are a common site in old redwood forests.

Fungi, such as these shelf mushrooms, are plentiful along woodland trails.

A deep creek runs beneath a wooden bridge at about 0.3 mile. An oak has fallen across the creek, but is still living.

About 200 yards past the footbridge there is an open canyon where the children can explore off the trail. There appears to be no poison oak here, but you should always check.

The trail turns and heads downhill just before 0.5 mile, and recrosses the creek from above on another footbridge. You can see that the canyon is wider and deeper here. Talk to the children about erosion and how creeks form canyons.

A large manzanita (the word means small apple in Spanish—if there are any fruit on the trees, have the children guess why it was named that) is beside the trail at about 0.6 mile. Have the children feel the smooth, hard wood and compare it to the madrone they felt earlier.

From 0.6 mile to the end there is chaparral on the downhill side of the trail and it is home to many small birds and rodents.

15. Zwierlein/Richard's Road/Dean Trails Loop

Type: Dayhike
Difficulty: Moderate for children
Distance: 2-mile loop
Hiking time: 2 hours
Elevation gain: 250 feet
Hikable: Year-round
Map: San Mateo County Park

While the Chickadee Trail provides a good introduction to the variety of plant communities found in Huddart County Park, this trail loop gives an in-depth look at the deep canyons where tall redwoods tower over an almost enchanted forest of ferns and low-lying plants. Between 1853 and 1860 five sawmills operated near the present-day boundaries of Huddart County Park, as the huge old-growth redwoods of the area were harvested to help meet the demand for lumber in booming San Francisco. It has been more than 100 years since the forests were logged, and much of the evidence of that activity is covered by the rejuvenated forest. A new forest of redwoods has grown up around the large stumps that are all that was left of the original virgin forests. A section of the trail on this hike, Richard's Road Trail, follows along the old road along

Footbridges are necessities for streams that become roaring torrents after heavy winter rains.

which the lumber was transported to Redwood City to waiting barges, which carried the lumber to San Francisco.

Follow the directions to hike 14, but continue past the first parking lot on the left to the Zwierlein Picnic Area. The trailhead is just to the south of the rest rooms.

Take the Zwierlein Trail to the right downhill through chaparral and into a small redwood grove. After about 0.1 mile the trail begins a series of sharp switchbacks down through an oak/madrone/bay forest. Some redwood rings where young trees have sprouted from the roots of an old stump are on the left side of the trail.

Many of the bay are multitrunked. Ask the children how they may have gotten that way. (Most of the young plants were eaten or broken off and new trunks were formed.)

There area also has many different types of large and small ferns along the trail. Have the children see how many they can spot.

The Zwierlein Trail continues downhill alongside a steadily deepening canyon until it dead ends into the Richard's Road Trail at about 0.5 mile. At this point take a left on Richard's Road Trail and head along the banks of West Union Creek. The trail is now a wide, well-maintained dirt road.

For the next 0.5 mile the trail leads by several rock outcroppings where you can take rest stops and look down over the creek, or scramble down the creekbank to explore the water's edge.

The canyon rises sharply to the left of the trail as you make a slow climb toward the confluence of West Union Creek and McGarvey Gulch Creek, which occurs at about 0.75 mile.

Several hundred yards past the confluence of the two creeks, Richard's Road Trail takes a sharp right turn across a large rock bridge to head up the hill on the opposite side of McGarvey Gulch Creek. Continue straight ahead here, as the trail becomes a narrow footpath heading upstream.

This is a good rest stop where the children have easy access to the creek.

After another 50 yards the Crystal Springs Trail crosses the creek to the right. Stay to the left on what is now Dean Trail. This trail immediately begins to head uphill on switchbacks. You are soon away from the creek and into a mixed forest with fir, oak, madrone, and bay.

At 1.75 miles the Zwierlein Trail leads off to the left. Take it and continue around the contour of the hill for 0.25 mile until you return to the trailhead.

16. Grabtown Gulch Trail Loop

Type: Dayhike
Difficulty: Difficult for children
Distance: 4-mile loop
Hiking time: 5 hours
Elevation gain: 1,200 feet
Hikable: Year-round
Map: Midpeninsula Regional Open
Space District

Its 2,511 acres and rugged terrain make Purisima Creek Redwoods Open Space Preserve ideal for those who want quiet solitude while enjoying strenuous hikes. It is the northernmost redwood forest in San Mateo County and is easily accessible to all of the urban and suburban sections of the San Francisco Peninsula. Three long ridges that divide the preserve into two large canyons extend west toward the ocean from Skyline Boulevard. Purisima Creek, one of the main attractions of the preserve, flows between Harkins and Tunitas ridges, and Whittemore Gulch, with

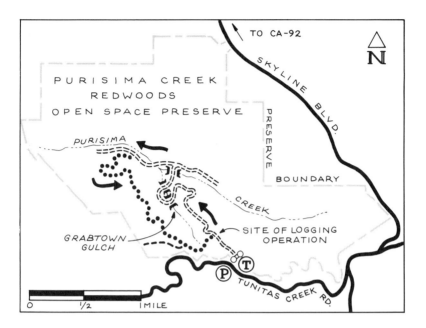

its seasonal creek that joins Purisima Creek at the west entrance to the preserve, lies to the north of Harkins Ridge. Most of the hikes within the preserve are very challenging, and beyond the capabilities of most children. There are several short trails near the west entrance off Higgins– Purisima Road where children can be introduced to the "enchanted forest" feel of the preserve. These can be explored before attempting the following hike, which is one of the less strenuous long hikes in the preserve.

The Grabtown Gulch trailhead is 2 miles west of Skyline Boulevard on Tunitas Creek Road. The brown metal gate that is common to Midpeninsula Regional Open Space District preserves is on the right side of the road. Several turnouts provide limited parking uphill from the gate.

This area was the first level spot that logging wagons reached on their 3- to 4-day trip from the docks at Redwood City to the sawmills along Purisima Creek. The trail starts off with a gentle rise along the slope of the ridge (this is probably the site of the Grabtown settlement), and comes to a small clearing in about 100 yards. Keep to the right at the first clearing, and continue along the trail to about 0.25 mile to a larger clearing. This was a landing area for logging operations in the last century. Have the children look around and try to imagine what the activity was like in the clearing during the peak logging years.

Trails lead out of the clearing to both the right and left. Take the right fork; you will return by the left.

The trail heads downhill through a forest of Douglas fir and young redwoods that reach above the tanoaks and madrone that grew on the

There are many types of ferns in redwood and bay forests.

hillsides after the earlier logging. There is still enough light to support a wild tangle of undergrowth of ceanothus, wild rose, toyon, and wild honeysuckle vines, but these will all disappear as the fir and redwood reach upward and form a canopy that will filter out all but a modest amount of light.

This area is an excellent study area of plant succession. Talk to your children about how different plant communities dominate in an area until what is called a climax community reaches full growth. Along this ridge the fir and redwood forests are the climax communities, but others replace them after destruction such as fire or logging. It then takes many years before the climax forests reach maturity.

The trail continues downhill along the side of the ridge until it crosses the ridge at about 1 mile, and begins a steep descent down into Grabtown Gulch. Along this west side of the ridge the trail is lined with ferns and other cool-loving plants. The creek is still some distance below the trail here, but you reach the shady banks of the creek at about 1.25 miles. In midsummer you will see colorful orange stands of 3-foot-tall tiger lilies.

At 1.5 miles Grabtown Gulch Creek enters Purisima Creek, and you cross an old logging bridge. This is the widest part of Purisima Canyon where shingle and saw mills flourished in the late 1800s. No sign of these is to be found today, however, as nature has begun its steady regeneration.

This is an excellent place to stop for lunch. The bridge is a good platform from which you can watch the creek flow beneath, and birds flitter in the growth along the bank. The children can explore along the creek except during times of high water.

The trail continues down the canyon, following the creek, and at about 1.75 miles a trail forks off to the left. Take this trail as it climbs the ridge to the west of Grabtown Gulch.

This long, steady climb follows the contours of the ridge, and offers good views of the creek below. The trail returns to the old logging landing at about 3.75 miles. Turn left at the landing to return to the parking area.

17. El Corte de Madera Creek Trail

Type: Dayhike
Difficulty: Moderate for children
Distance: 2 miles round trip
Hiking time: 2 hours
Elevation gain: 300 feet
Hikable: Year-round
Map: Midpeninsula Regional Open
Space District

El Corte de Madera Creek rises from springs near Skyline Boulevard, and flows between high ridges along the west side of El Corte de Madera Open Space Preserve. This preserve, with elevations ranging from the 2,400-foot summit of Sierra Morena to the 700-foot elevation at the bottom

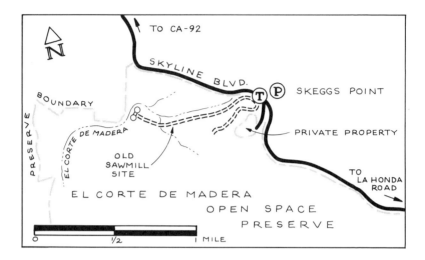

of the canyon where the creek leaves the preserve on the west side, is a place of deep canyons and exposed ridges. The high ridges and deep canyons offer contrasting, but equally breathtaking, views. The redwood forests were first logged in the 1860s and logging continued until the late 1980s when the Open Space District acquired the 2,700 acres.

 Park on the east side of Skyline Boulevard near Skeggs Point 3 miles north of CA-84 and walk 300 yards north. Cross the road to the preserve entrance.

Take the dirt service road to the right (not the paved private road to the left), and head uphill. The road makes a sharp turn after about 100 yards and forks. Take the fork to the right, which heads downhill.

You are now on the old El Corte de Madera Creek Road. As you continue downhill you pass through an area where signs of logging still abound, but by 0.5 mile you reach a forest of fir and redwood that stands high above the creek.

At about 0.75 mile a small creek comes into El Corte de Madera Creek from the left. This was the site of one of the earliest sawmills in the canyon, which operated in the 1860s. This is a good place for a rest stop and a picnic. You can talk to your children about the logging activities of the late 1800s and how logging practices have changed in the past century. The children can also explore the creekbanks here.

As the road goes farther into the cool, moist canyon the ferns grow taller by the creek, and brilliant red and orange wildflowers can be seen on the creekbanks from May through August.

The road comes to a gate at about 1 mile, and hikers may not go any farther on the road. Return to the parking area by the same route.

18. Alambique/Loop Trails

Type: Dayhike
Difficulty: Moderate for children
Distance: 1.7-mile loop
Hiking time: 1 hour
Elevation gain: 150 feet
Hikable: Year-round
Map: San Mateo County Park

The old roads that remain from more than a century of logging and ranching on the 942 acres of Wunderlich County Park form the basis of the 15 miles of well-laid-out trails that crisscross meadows and steep hillsides. The hillsides were heavily logged during the 1850s and 1860s, and the lower hills and meadows were farmed after the timber had been

Fire-scarred stumps offer children a place to play as they imagine trolls and other forest denizens.

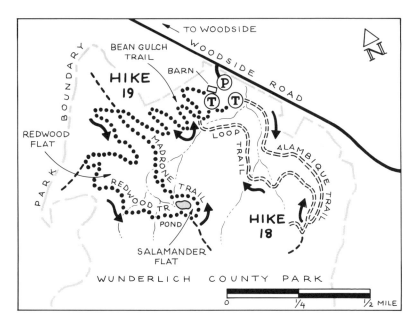

cleared. The steeper hillsides returned to their natural states as redwoods and tanbark oak sprouted from the stumps of the earlier growth. The wide trails of Wunderlich are popular with equestrians, and hikers are warned to stand quietly on the upper side of the trail as horses and their riders pass by. Alambique Creek and its tributaries flow out of the many springs found on the hillsides.

Take the Woodside exit off I-280, and head southwest on Woodside Road (CA-84) for 2 miles. The small sign that marks the entrance to the park is on the right-hand side of the road. Continue to the parking lot just below the large barn. The trailhead for Alambique Trail is to the left from the parking lot.

This is an old ranch road that leads through a tunnel formed by oaks that have grown over the road. The old road heads slowly uphill above an open field below. Large eucalyptus and Monterey pine grow on the sides of the road along this section. Have the children look at the vast piles of shredded bark and fallen leaves that litter the hillsides beneath the eucalyptus. Explain that in areas with little rainfall or summer fog, this litter becomes extremely combustible and is a real fire hazard.

After about 0.25 mile the trail takes a sharp turn to the left and narrows to a footpath.

As you get higher the vegetation changes somewhat and there are fewer exotics, although there are still a number of large old eucalyptus. There are more fir and oak, as well as the beginning of redwood.

At 0.75 mile the narrow trail begins a short, steep ascent, and joins with another wide ranch road. Take a sharp right turn here and begin the trek back downhill along the Trail Loop.

Uphill from the trail there are several monstrous eucalyptus trees, and at about 1 mile the road crosses over several good-sized creeks that have carved canyons in the hillsides. The shaded slopes are covered by a good stand of second-growth redwood. The children can explore along the banks of the creeks, which are often dry, where the road crosses them, but there is not much to find since the water seldom stands. It is either rushing pell-mell down the canyon or is not there. Have the children discuss why this makes for little growth along the path of the creek.

(e)

At about 1.5 miles the Trail Loop crosses the Bear Gulch Trail. You may either continue straight on the Trail Loop, which winds back to the park office at the old barn, or take a right on the Bear Gulch Trail and head more directly back to the barn. Both choices are about the same distance.

19. Bear Gulch/Redwood/Madrone Trails Loop

Type:	Dayhike
Difficulty:	Difficult for children
Distance:	3-mile loop
Hiking time:	2 hours
Elevation gain:	600 feet
Hikable:	Year-round
Map:	San Mateo County Park

While hike 18 took you through a mixed forest along the southeast side of the Wunderlich County Park and back around the edge of a ridge through second-growth redwoods, this hike follows the northern boundary of the park through chaparral and mixed conifer forest to Redwood Flat. There the trail leads to Salamander Flat before heading back downhill through a dense grove of redwoods. Alambique Creek was the primary source of water for early settlers in the area, and they eventually built a reservoir at Salamander Flat. Water was then piped downhill to the residents. Today the reservoir is a picnic site and salamander breeding ground rather than a water supply, and hikers are often surprised to come upon the sheltered pond as they hike along the ridge.

Follow directions for hike 18 to the parking lot at Wunderlich County Park. The trailhead for this hike is located uphill from the parking lot behind the large old barn.

The Bear Gulch Trail begins a steep ascent with switchbacks up through a mixed oak and madrone forest. Some chaparral can be seen on the downhill side of the trail. This is a favorite equestrian trail, and it can be a bit narrow when you meet a large horse on one of the switchbacks. Remind your children about getting out of the way and not making any quick movements that might spook the horses.

At about 0.5 mile the Bear Gulch Trail crosses the Madrone Trail. Horses aren't allowed on Bear Gulch Trail past Madrone Trail during the winter months, and that makes the trail more enjoyable for hikers. Between 0.5 and 1 mile the trail winds upward at a steady pace, and through a good grove of second-growth redwood. At about 0.75 mile there are remains of several very large redwood stumps left from some long-ago forest fire. Children often like to play in these and pretend they are forts, etc.

Near 1 mile a spur leads off to the right of the main trail, but keep to the left as the trail approaches a road outside the park boundaries.

Ponds, such as this one at Salamander Flat, are always a good place to rest and explore.

Just past 1 mile at Redwood Flat, Redwood Trail leads off to the left. Take this trail as it winds around the contour of the canyons. For the next 0.5 mile the trail is fairly level but windy. Steep canyons are on the left side of the trail as it passes through large redwoods.

At Salamander Flat at 1.5 miles there is a pleasant surprise for all. A good-sized reservoir that once served residents below it now sits, full, on the left side of the trail just before the junction with the Madrone Trail. It is not a swimming hole, for the sides drop off quickly to deep water, but it is an excellent picnic site where the children can search for the many salamanders that can be found there at various times of the year. This was a favorite breeding spot for them even before the reservoir was built.

As you leave the reservoir, head downhill on the Madrone Trail. It winds steadily down through large stands of redwoods that furnish cool shade and moisture for the many ferns and other shade-loving plants. Large redwoods often capture their own water from the summer fogs that frequently cover the hills and mountains around the San Francisco Bay. This captured water is often equal to an additional 8 to 10 inches of rain a year.

Just before 2.75 miles you reach the intersection of the Madrone Trail with the Bear Gulch Trail. Take a right onto the Bear Gulch Trail to return to the barn.

20. Meadows Trail Loop

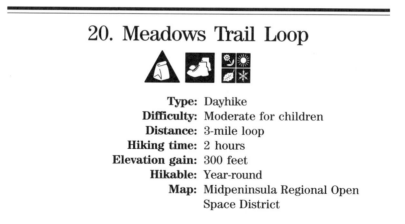

Type: Dayhike
Difficulty: Moderate for children
Distance: 3-mile loop
Hiking time: 2 hours
Elevation gain: 300 feet
Hikable: Year-round
Map: Midpeninsula Regional Open Space District

La Honda Creek Open Space Preserve includes nearly 400 acres of steep slopes covered with thick forests and open grasslands. The preserve is located in a remote area that is not easily reached, and this has kept the plant communities there relatively undisturbed. There are special access conditions at the preserve, and hikers are requested to contact the Midpeninsula Regional Open Space District office at 415-949-5500

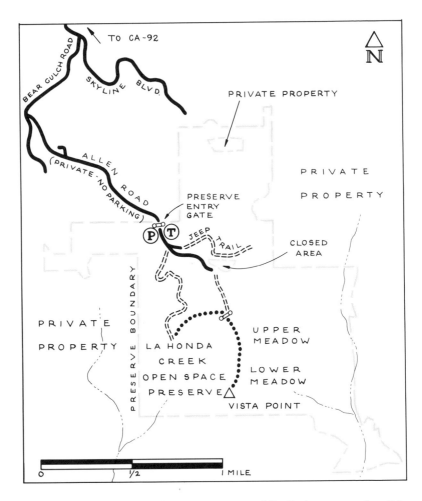

before visiting the park. This remoteness and limited access makes this preserve an ideal one for hikers who wish to observe wildlife, and it is well worth the effort to obtain a permit for hiking in the preserve.

Directions for access to the preserve are given along with the permit.

Head east on the paved road as it climbs a slight rise. You pass through a small redwood grove and a clearing with some very large Douglas fir around it.

At about 0.25 mile the road intersects with another. Continue straight, passing south of an old barn and caretaker's cottage. Uphill from the road is private land and hikers should not venture there.

The paved road ends at about 0.5 mile, and ranch roads fork off to the left and right. Take the road to the right as it heads downhill between the barn and a corral. Continue through a wooden gate to the meadow at about 0.75 mile.

As you pass through the gate a breathtaking view of the ridges and open grasslands to the west open up, and the ocean can be seen in the far distance. You are confronted with a dark wall of oak, fir, and redwood as you turn to the east. The road turns into a narrow trail as you pass through the meadow.

At just under 1 mile the trail enters a small forest at the bottom of the sloping meadow. There are several ancient redwoods here that were not logged in even the early years. Have the children compare these with the second-growth redwoods they have passed on the trail. These trees are probably more than 1,000 years old, and the second-growth ones are just over 100 years old. Look for signs of age other than the size of the trunks and the height of the trees. **e**

Redwoods and other large trees often show damage from long-ago storms.

The trail soon passes through this small grove, and enters another meadow. The views are just as dramatic here as on the upper meadow, and both meadows are carpeted with brilliant wildflower blooms in the spring.

The trail ends as you enter the lower meadow, as a dense forest blocks your progress on one side, and a precipitous slope that leads down to the canyon of Harrington Creek blocks you on the other. This meadow is an excellent picnic area as the children can explore the plant life in the meadow and along its edges as the adults enjoy the views.

Return to the upper meadow after your break, and take the trail that leads to the left from the meadow toward a service road on the west side of the preserve about half-way up the slope. The trail heads down a ridge and connects with the service road at about 2 miles.

Turn right and take the service road uphill. This takes you on a gradual uphill climb through alternate woodlands of oak, madrone, fir, and redwood, and clearings that are covered with low-lying brush and open grassland. In the forests you can see large redwood stumps, some more than 5 feet across, that are reminders of the towering old-growth forests that were logged in the 1800s. Watch for circles of second-growth redwoods that have sprouted from the roots surrounding these large stumps. Point out the regenerative powers of the redwoods.

At about 2.5 miles the trail comes out into a clearing below an open hillside and above the deep, wooded canyon that Harrington Creek drains through. Continue around the bend to the parking area.

21. Cooley Landing Trail Loop

Type: Dayhike
Difficulty: Easy for children
Distance: 1.5-mile loop
Hiking time: 1 hour
Elevation gain: None
Hikable: Year-round
Maps: USGS topographics—Palo Alto and Mountain View

There are more than 2 miles of broad marshes that extend from Menlo Park to Palo Alto along the shores of the San Francisco Bay. A number of paths, boardwalks, and viewing platforms have been built to

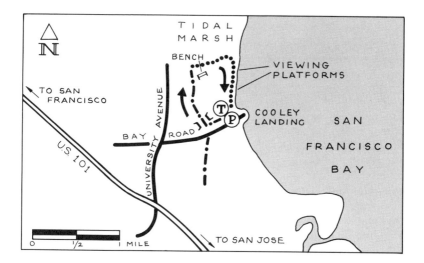

allow hikers and walkers to enjoy the views, and to observe closeup the plant and animal life that abounds in tidal marshes and mudflats. Cooley Landing in east Palo Alto is one of the few areas of this marshland that has been restored. There a boardwalk and paths lead you through and around tidal marshes, open water, and a slough where you have an excellent opportunity to view a wide variety of birdlife.

Take the University Avenue exit north off US 101 in Palo Alto. After less than 0.5 mile, turn right on Bay Road, and head east until the road dead ends at the parking area at Cooley Landing.

Start this trail along the dikes of the salt pond on the north side of the slough at the plaza at Cooley Landing. Begin by heading west on Bay Road away from the bay for about 200 yards. Cross the bridge over the slough to your right and follow the levee straight ahead. The levee bends as it follows around the slough, and to your right is one of the many salt ponds that were built in the south San Francisco Bay during the late 1800s and early 1900s. This one is being restored to a tidal marsh by the Midpeninsula Regional Open Space District.

The path is paved until 0.75 mile. At the end of the pavement there is a bench in a bend of the levee. This is a good place for a rest stop, where the children can explore along the edges of the levee and see what small animals and birds live nearby.

The clapper rail is a well-camouflaged waterbird that is exciting to see, for it is endangered and is protected by the various preserves and refuges around the bay.

The path narrows as it continues around the levee (it will be widened to 8 feet in the early 1990s to accommodate bicycles), and you should stay on the path that circles the outer levee to continue the loop.

Marshlands frequently offer surprises to silent hikers.

Just before and just after 1 mile there are two viewing platforms with benches where you can stop to watch the waterfowl and shorebirds that feed here. At low tide there are many more long-legged wading birds hunting for shrimp and mollusks.

Complete the loop along the levee around the slough to the bridge where you began.

22. Windy Hill Summit Trail Loop

Type: Dayhike
Difficulty: Easy for children
Distance: 0.75-mile loop
Hiking time: 1 hour
Elevation gain: 130 feet
Hikable: Year-round
Map: Midpeninsula Regional Open
Space District

The Windy Hill Open Space Preserve includes two bald knobs that stand high above Portola Valley. Hikers who climb the short trail to the top of the bald knobs have a 360-degree view of the Pacific, the San Francisco Bay, distant mountains, and many cities. In the summer, wind and fog are common occurrences here, and the views are blocked by the fog banks at times, but a visit to this preserve is always bracing and invigorating. Some 14 miles of trails traverse the 1,131-acre preserve, crossing grass-covered meadows, climbing steep slopes to ridgelines, and following stream canyons, but the short trail to the top of the bald knobs is one of the most popular, and gives a good overview of the 8.5-mile Windy Hill Trail Loop, one of the longest loop trails on the peninsula.

The main entrance to the preserve is located on the east side of Skyline Boulevard 2 miles south of La Honda Road. The trailhead is on the north side of the picnic area.

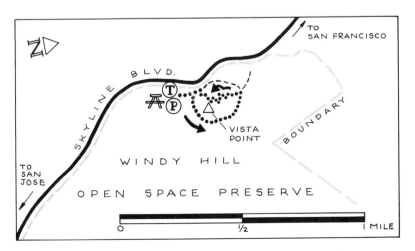

There are a number of longer hikes in this preserve, but this short loop takes you to a top-of-the-world view of the San Francisco Bay Area. Take the trail to the left from the Skyline Boulevard picnic area toward the knobs of Windy Hill. This is a well-marked trail, and the knobs are in view the whole time.

The knobs are open, grass-covered landmarks, and on the less than 0.5-mile trail to the top, many San Francisco region peaks come into view. At the top you can see Black Mountain, Mount Hamilton, Mount Diablo, and Mount Tamalpais.

In addition, you can see the ocean to the west, and the San Francisco Bay, with its many surrounding cities, to the east.

Have the children try to pick out some of the peaks and cities, and if you live within view, try to find your neighborhood.

Return to the parking lot by the same trail you came, or take the one down the opposite side of the knobs for a loop.

Children love to come unexpectedly upon great climbing spots such as these rocks.

23. North Ridge Trail Loop

Type:	Dayhike
Difficulty:	Moderate for children
Distance:	2.5-mile loop
Hiking time:	2 hours
Elevation gain:	400 feet
Hikable:	Year-round
Map:	Midpeninsula Regional Open Space District

The deep canyons of Mindego Creek form the centerpiece of the Russian Ridge Open Space Preserve, and 2,572-foot Borel Hill is its high point. Trails run along the ridges that parallel Skyline Boulevard and to the peak of Borel Hill, and ranch roads lead down the west slopes of

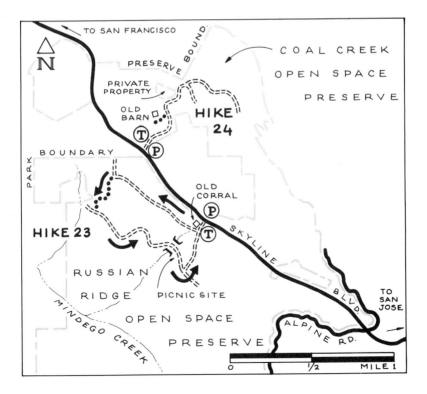

Separate the tall, dry grasses of early summer and you may find glorious spots of color.

the hills to the canyon floors. Views to the east cover the San Francisco Bay and the hills of the East Bay, and those to the west include expanses of ridges all the way to the ocean.

Park at the Caltrans Vista Point on Skyline Boulevard 1 mile north of Alpine Road. Cross the road to the entrance stile.

Head straight ahead on the old ranch road. A trail heading north and south crosses the old ranch road just beyond the remains of an old corral. Turn right on this trail to head north. The trail makes a gentle climb along the rock-covered crest of the ridge, and there are fantastic views to the east of the South Bay and the East Bay hills beyond. To the west, ranchlands and ridges stretch all the way to the ocean.

The large hill to the southeast is Mindego Hill. Its large bulk and flattened top stand out against the dark ridges behind. Mindego is of volcanic origin, and was probably formed more than 135 million years ago. Over time the ridges and peaks around Mindego have eroded into only remnants of their previous size, and the rounded mountains have been home to numerous cattle ranches over the past century.

Continue along the ridge north toward the preserve's northern boundary, where a radio broadcasting antenna stands. Far below you can see the old ranch road that you will use for your return to the parking area.

At just under 1 mile a lightly marked trail (although by the time this book reaches you, the trail may have been completed and widened) takes off downhill. This is just before the preserve boundary. The trail makes a long switchback as it heads downhill, and there are views of a heavily wooded canyon of a branch of Mindego Creek that flows into Alpine Creek.

Have the children watch for herds of deer that live in the woods below and come out into the meadows to forage for food. If you are quiet you can often watch them for extended periods of time. They quickly disappear back into the woods when they become aware of you.

Meadowlarks and other songbirds are often seen in this area also.

At about 1.25 miles the trail reaches the lower ranch road. Turn left on the road and begin a long, gentle climb back to the parking lot.

At about 1.75 miles the road heads into a wooded ravine and crosses a spring-fed tributary of Mindego Creek. The children can explore along the creek here, and climb around the large lichen-covered outcroppings under the old, wind-shorn fir trees at about 2 miles.

At 2.25 miles you leave the forest of fir trees and enter a small, protected meadow that is full of wildflowers in the spring. This secluded, tree-bordered shelter is an excellent picnic spot. The children can explore along the border of the meadow where the trees begin, to see what evidence of small animals they can find and to look for the many birds that live and feed along the meadow boundary.

After this rest stop return to the trail, take the trail to the left about 200 yards past the picnic site, and continue to the parking area at 2.5 miles.

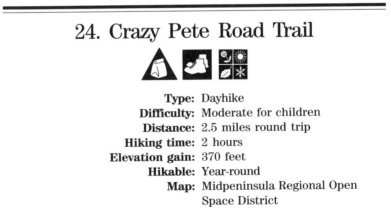

24. Crazy Pete Road Trail

Type: Dayhike
Difficulty: Moderate for children
Distance: 2.5 miles round trip
Hiking time: 2 hours
Elevation gain: 370 feet
Hikable: Year-round
Map: Midpeninsula Regional Open
Space District

Coal Creek Open Space Preserve is almost surrounded by Russian Ridge, Monte Bello, and Skyline Ridge preserves, and Windy Hill is just south of it. The main attractions of the preserve are three meadows that lie just below Skyline Ridge. These are a palette of color during the spring bloom, and they are bordered by groves of oak and madrone. The head-

Thistles are often thought of as weeds, but they are also a beautiful spring wildflower.

waters for two large creeks are located within the preserve also.

There is limited parking at the Crazy Pete Road entrance 6 miles south of La Honda Road on Skyline Boulevard. The trail heads out from the parking area onto Crazy Pete Road.

The trail leads out into a pasture area, and crosses open grassland that is covered with wildflowers during the spring bloom. Those who like to paint, photograph, or just enjoy wildflowers will be thrilled with the show here. You may want to bring a flower guidebook to help you identify the many different small flowers. Remember, don't pick, just look. This is a preserve where all plants and animals are protected.

At just under 0.5 mile, near an old barn, you can take a trail spur to the left and head downhill a short way to where you can enjoy a picnic or rest stop in a bright, open meadow. Have the children look for very tiny flowers that provide colorful highlights to the green pasture. There should also be plenty of small insects and creepy crawlies that they can observe through view boxes or with magnifying glasses. They also like to look at the many flowers with the magnifying glasses. Have them see if they can spot any tiny insects that may be pollinating the flowers.

By the time this guide is published, there may be a trail that leads through the meadow to Mount Melville to the north.

After a stop in the meadow, you can return to the trail and head past the barn on Crazy Pete Road. The road jogs around a private inholding at about 0.75 mile, and it offers fine views of El Corte de Madera Creek Canyon as it passes through woodlands with live oak and madrone.

At just over 1 mile the trail passes the private land to the left and begins a slight descent. A service road leads off to the right, but veer left to stay on Crazy Pete Road. At about 1.25 miles you come to a small knoll in the middle of a clearing. The noonday sun warms this meadow, and the knoll is an excellent place to have a lunch before you head back up the trail.

Return to the parking area by the same route.

Look along the floors of redwood forests for the bright green of redwood sorrel. This plant is also known for its sour-tasting leaves.

25. Horseshoe Lake Trail Loop

Type: Dayhike
Difficulty: Easy for children
Distance: 1.5-mile loop
Hiking time: 1 hour
Elevation gain: 100 feet
Hikable: Year-round
Map: Midpeninsula Regional Open
Space District

Another of the multitude of open space preserves and parks found along Skyline Boulevard, Skyline Ridge Open Space Preserve has 1,200 acres that include a Christmas tree farm, two small reservoirs, and a 2,493-foot knoll that is unnamed. The upper regions of the preserve are covered by rolling grasslands, and the steep slopes of the lower regions are covered by mixed conifer forests. Native Americans lived in the region and gathered acorns from the oak forests. Some of the bedrock grinding stones they used to grind the acorns can still be seen in the preserve. Settlers came to the area as early as 1850 and built ranch houses along the ridge.

Park at the preserve entrance located on Skyline Boulevard just less than 1 mile southeast of Alpine Road. Take the old farm road that heads downhill from the parking area.

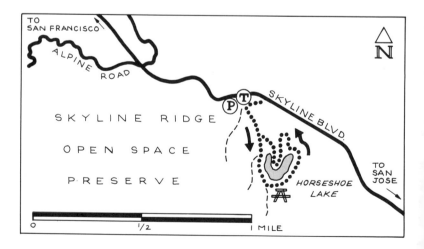

The road descends into a small valley that lies to the east of the steep slopes that drop down from the preserve's summit. The road goes through open grassland that has an occasional oak, and you can soon see the U-shaped Horseshoe Lake that wraps around a knoll with trees jutting from its top.

At 0.5 mile the road ends and trails fork to the right and left. Take the right and continue for 200 yards to the south end of the lake. Cross the earthen dam and take the path around the marsh at the rim of the lake. The children can explore along the edges of this marsh for signs of wildlife, and look for small birds that live there. During nesting season in particular you should see and hear a number of birds, including redwing blackbirds. Frogs abound here also.

In early morning or evening you may see deer, raccoon, fox, and maybe even a bobcat as they come to drink at the lake. These animals inhabit the surrounding woods and aren't often seen except at the lake and in the open meadows.

At 0.75 mile the trail leads to the top of the knoll, where picnic tables sit. There you can have a pleasant break as the children explore around the lake.

After you have rested, continue on around the knoll on the trail to the dam, and return by the same route.

Man-made lakes soon fit into the natural settings of peninsula parks.

26. Big Tree Trail

Type: Dayhike
Difficulty: Moderate for children
Distance: 1.5-mile loop
Hiking time: 1 hour
Elevation gain: 250 feet
Hikable: Year-round
Map: San Mateo County Park

Sam McDonald County Park is part of the much larger park complex that includes Pescadero Creek County Park, Memorial County Park, Heritage Grove Redwood Preserve, and Portola State Park. All of these include nearly 10,000 acres of redwood and mixed conifer forests, steep canyons carved by roaring streams, and miles of trails. The streams are lush with stands of ferns, and the ridges and high meadows are covered with rolling grasslands and chaparral, and have abundant wildflowers during the spring. Wildlife is plentiful throughout the parks, but more so in the high meadows and chaparral country. Some of the largest coast redwoods in the San Francisco Bay region can be found in the groves of these parks.

Park in the parking area at the ranger station of Sam McDonald County Park off Pescadero Road about 0.5 mile west of the junction of Pescadero and Alpine roads.

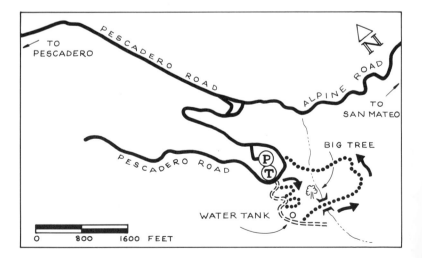

Decay is part of the continuing cycle of nature.

From the parking lot take the trail that crosses over Pescadero Road to the Big Tree Trail. Be careful crossing the road, since there are curves on both sides of the crosswalk.

The trail begins on the fire road that heads uphill, and during the first 0.25 mile crosses over the road several times. Sometimes it follows the road, and others it becomes a narrow trail alongside it.

Along this section there a number of good-sized redwoods, and old stumps of even larger ones that were cut down during the late 1800s. Have the children explore some of the old stumps, and see if they can guess how old they may have been when they were cut. Guestimates can be made on the number of rings that one can count within say 5 inches, and then interpolating that into the number that might be in the whole stump.

The trail climbs steadily here, and at about 0.5 mile the road passes by a large water tank on the left; the trail leads off the road to the left into large redwoods just past the tank. This is the real beginning of the Big Tree Trail loop, and this is where you will find the largest of the large. The trail follows the contour of the hills along this section, and stays relatively level.

At just past 0.75 mile you round a curve in the trail and come upon what is probably the largest redwood tree found in this grove—maybe even one of the largest found in San Mateo County.

You are uphill from it as it rises from the creekbed below, and you can see that even one of its limbs, which grows upward like a trunk, is as large as many of the second-growth redwood in the park. A bench is located beside the trail so that you can sit, look, and wonder about the life span of this magnificent tree.

Just past the bench the trail curves to the left, begins to descend, and crosses a footbridge over the creek. It climbs again on the other side and you have another view of the huge redwood. From this side you can see where it rises from the ground, which makes it seem even larger.

By 1 mile the trail heads downhill as it leads through a more open understory. It winds its way around the contour of the hill, and returns to Pescadero Road at just under 1.5 miles. Cross the road and return to the parking area.

27. Mount Ellen Nature Trail

Type: Dayhike
Difficulty: Moderate for children
Distance: 1 mile
Hiking time: 1 hour
Elevation gain: 300 feet
Hikable: Year-round
Map: San Mateo County Park

Memorial County Park is the oldest unit in the San Mateo County Park system. It was acquired in 1924 as a memorial to the men of San Mateo County who lost their lives in World War I. It is exhibiting degradation because of its long history and overuse, but its trails still offer excellent introductions to the varied and complex natural history of the Santa Cruz Mountains.

Park in the lot at the park entrance and ranger station off Pescadero Road about 3.5 miles west of the junction of Pescadero and Alpine roads. Pick up a self-guiding brochure to the Mount Ellen Nature Trail at the visitor center just inside the park before crossing Pescadero Road to the beginning of the Mount Ellen Nature Trail.

This self-guided nature trail begins with a gentle climb through a

The immensity of coast redwoods is almost incomprehensible to those who have not seen them close up.

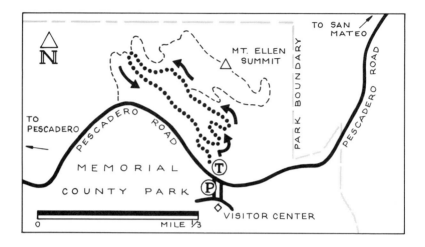

batch of redwood forest understory, with huckleberry bushes, some brambles, and ferns. After about 0.1 mile it begins a series of switchbacks uphill through second-growth redwoods, some of which form almost perfect circles around old stumps. Have the children discuss how these circles of trees formed (sprouted from the roots of old trees that were cut or died). Mention that these can be found throughout redwood forests, and that they are only one of several ways that redwoods regenerate. The others include sprouting from seeds and growing directly from the stumps.

One of the best examples of these redwood circles is found at just before 0.25 mile. The children can climb uphill from the trail to stand in the midst of the circle and look skyward to get a good feel of the height of the trees.

Just past 0.25 mile the trail turns sharply to the left and follows a fairly straight and level path along the side of the hill through a mixed forest of redwood, fir, madrone, and oak. Just before 0.5 mile the trail to the top of Mount Ellen takes off to the right. This loop adds a little over 0.5 mile and about 300 feet to the hike. If your children would like to climb to the peak, take this trail; otherwise, keep straight ahead to continue the nature trail loop.

Around 0.75 mile several seasonal creeks cross the trail, and some large trees that have been uprooted by the roaring waters during winter storms are beside the trail. Ask the children how these trees were uprooted, and explain to them about the power of rushing water.

The trail continues around the hill and takes a sharp turn back to the trailhead just past 0.75 mile. The return trail follows above a canyon where large bay and redwood are located.

Return to the parking area across the road after reaching the trailhead.

28. Pescadero Marsh Trail Loop

Type: Dayhike
Difficulty: Easy for children
Distance: 1.75-mile loop
Hiking time: 1 hour
Elevation gain: Minimal
Hikable: Year-round
Map: Butano State Park

Pescadero Marsh Natural Preserve is more than 500 acres of coastal wetlands, the largest wetland area between San Francisco Bay and Elkhorn Slough near Watsonville. More than 100 species of animals and 380 species of plants are found in the marsh area, and many migrating birds use the marsh as a layover point as they fly along the Pacific Flyway each fall and spring. The marsh was formed about 6,500 years ago at the end of the last Ice Age, and the first humans to inhabit the area around the marsh were the Ohlone Indians. They were part of a group of Native Americans who lived between what is now Monterey and San Francisco as long 10,000 years ago. They used the marsh and surrounding country as a source of a variety of food such as wild herbs, clams, fish, shellfish,

Pescadero Marsh offers easy trails into one of nature's richest nurseries.

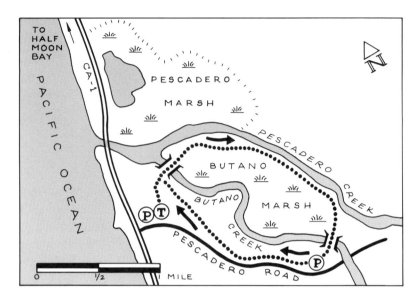

elk, deer, and sea mammals. When the first Spanish explorers came to the area in 1774, thousands of trout and salmon swam in the streams and marsh. Wolf and grizzly bear stalked the forests on the surrounding hills. By the 1850s a small town was established southeast of the marsh, and human activity has continued in the region ever since.

The marsh lies at the northeast corner of CA-1 and Pescadero Road 17 miles south of Half Moon Bay. For this hike, park in the pullout along the north side of Pescadero Road about 200 yards off CA-1. The trail leads out of the rear of the pullout.

The first 0.25 mile of the trail leads through a covering of coastal scrub where many small birds flit about. At 0.25 mile the trail comes to an end at a larger, better maintained one. Take a left, and head over the wooden footbridge across Butano Creek.

For the next 0.75 mile the trail leads along a levee through the marshland. Have the children keep a lookout for small mammals such as muskrats and raccoon, especially during the spring mating season. Also have them look for the small tepeelike nests of the muskrats beside the water.

Waterfowl and shorebirds feed in the marsh and open water along the levee. Keep an eye out for different types of waterfowl, and maybe keep count of how many different types you spot. Although it is interesting to know the names of the different birds, and you can bring a bird guide with you to assist in this, it is not necessary. You can have fun just looking for different ones.

Another thing to keep an eye out for along the levee is the different plant growth as you go farther up the creek away from the ocean. Some plants can survive in the brackish water (mixture of saltwater and freshwater) closer to the ocean, while others can survive only in freshwater.

At about 0.75 mile the levee takes a sharp turn to the right, and heads back toward Pescadero Road. There is a thicker growth of tules and other marsh plants here. Look for smaller birds such as the redwing blackbird along this stretch. Discuss why there are some small trees such as willow along this stretch when there weren't before. (This is past the normal reaches of the brackish water, which willow and most other small trees can't tolerate.)

At about 1 mile the trail leaves the marsh and enters a parking lot near Pescadero Road where there are rest rooms. Take a sharp right turn out of the parking lot to return on the trail uphill from the marsh.

Along this section of trail, which is bordered by coastal scrub, there are many more small birds. You also may see some small mammals.

The trail here also offers a better view of the marshland you have just passed through, since it is somewhat higher.

At 1.5 mile you return to the trail that leads back to the parking area. Turn left and return through the coastal scrub.

---

29. Butano Creek Trail Loop

Type: Dayhike
Difficulty: Moderate to difficult for children
Distance: 2.5-mile loop
Hiking time: 3 hours
Elevation gain: 400 feet
Hikable: Year-round
Map: Butano State Park

The 2,186 acres of redwoods in Butano State Park were destined to be logged in the 1950s when conservationists joined together in a successful fight to preserve this outstanding grove. The steep canyons in the park are covered with majestic redwoods that provide shade for the many ferns and other shade-loving plants commonly found in redwood forests. In the winter this area is often the scene of heavy rains, and the creeks fill with roiling water carrying debris, limbs, and small logs. Some winters, even large logs cascade down the canyons, wiping out small trees and bridges as the swift-moving streams rise above normal levels. The evidence of this power can be seen along the Butano Creek Trail.

From CA-1 take Pescadero Road 2.5 miles to Cloverdale Road. Turn south on Cloverdale Road and continue for 4.5 miles to the park entrance. Once in the park continue on the main paved road for just under 1 mile to a turnout on the left side of the road at the Butano Creek trailhead.

Take a left from the parking area as the trail leads up Butano Creek. Have the children discuss some of the ways you can tell which direction a stream or creek is flowing. They may wish to drop a leaf in the water to make sure you are heading upstream.

For the first 0.25 mile you walk with the creek on your left, and then you cross over to the other side on a wooden footbridge. This bridge is occasionally washed out by floodwaters. Have the children try to imagine how the water must appear during such times, and discuss what damage could be done along the banks of the creeks and on the slopes above.

The trail continues along the creek until 0.75 mile and passes by numerous large redwoods and many signs of flood damage. This damage includes large trees uprooted on the hillsides and logs that have stuck in curves of the creek as they were pushed downstream during the floods.

At about 0.75 mile the trail crosses the creek in several places that are impassable during high water, making this portion of the trail inaccessible after heavy winter rains. Some bridges in this section are portable ones that are taken down after the rains begin and are replaced after the water level lowers in the spring or early summer.

Just before 1 mile the trail leads away from the creek and quickly climbs the steep slope above the creek. Have the children be cautious

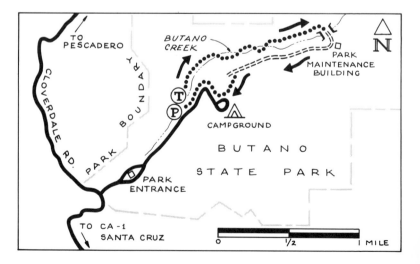

Heavy winter rains make for luxurious growth beneath the redwoods along Butano Creek.

along some stretches here, since a slip off the side of the trail can lead to a tumble down the slope for several hundred feet.

Just past 1 mile the trail descends to the creek again, and crosses it on a large bridge that was once used by loggers. The trail continues on a logging road and makes a steady climb to the top of the ridge far above the creek below. The forests here are more mixed than the redwood and bay forests by the creek, and they have a more open understory.

At about 1.25 miles the road passes by a building used by the park maintenance staff, then levels out, and begins a slow descent. Just past 1.5 miles you pass a trail that leads off to the left to the campground. Several hundred yards later you enter a portion of the campground before joining the paved road that leads back to the parking area.

Continue downhill on the paved road as it winds below the campground to the trailhead on Butano Creek at about 2.5 miles.

30. Bean Hollow Beach Trail

Type: Dayhike
Difficulty: Easy for children
Distance: 2 miles round trip
Hiking time: 2 hours
Elevation gain: Minimal
Hikable: Year-round
Map: Bean Hollow State Beach

Some of the most spectacular rock and surf scenery along the northern section of California's central coast is found along this hike. While there are no large sandy beaches, there is a small intimate one at the southern terminus of the trail, and there are wave-battered rocks, some tide pools, and an excellent view of a harbor seal rookery along the shore. The coast along here is comprised of sandstone and an unusual rocky material known as the Pigeon Point Formation. This 65 million- to 70 million-year-old formation is a tough, erosion-resistant conglomerate of rock and sand that extends from Pescadero Creek to Ano Nuevo Point.

You can park at either end of the trail, but I prefer to park at the southern end where the small cove with Bean Hollow State Beach is located. The trail heads north along the beach from this parking lot.

The self-guided trail leads north from the beach, and climbs up on the marine terrace at about 0.25 mile. The trail leads along the edge of this terrace, which is covered by coastal scrub. Since the winds and

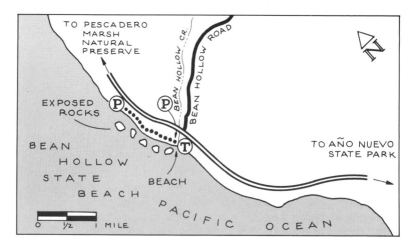

Wind and surf etch unusual markings on seashore rocks.

waves along the shoreline here combine the salt spray with the air, plants that grow on the terrace must be salt-tolerant. This limits the plants that can survive here.

Offshore between 0.25 mile and 0.5 mile are a number of wave-battered rocks that are covered with white material. This is guano, or excrement, from cormorants and other ocean-feeding birds that roost there. During low tide you can often see large groups of these birds resting on the rocks. They frequently have their wings spread wide to dry them off after diving for fish.

Between 0.5 mile and 0.75 mile the rocks and reefs offshore are often covered with lazing harbor seals. These seals feed on fish below and then return to the exposed rocks to rest and digest their meals. Young males can frequently be seen jousting for position on the rocks. The seals are safe from sharks and any other ocean predators while they are out of the sea.

The steep cliffs between 0.75 mile and 1 mile are a good example of how erosion removes hundreds of acres of land from the shoreline of California each year. Softer cliffs can erode up to 20 feet in one year, while hard ones like those at Bean Hollow may only erode 6 inches. Most of this erosion takes place during the high waves of winter storms. There are several gullies along this last section of trail where you can see how high the waves reach during the winter. Have the children guess how far the waves reach, and estimate how far that is from the normal high tide mark far below.

The trail ends at 1 mile. Return to Bean Hollow Beach Cove where Bean Hollow Creek enters the ocean.

Santa Clara County

Grandfather and grandson share the enjoyment of hiking.

31. Corte Madera/Meadowlark/Acorn Trails Loop

Type:	Dayhike
Difficulty:	Difficult for children
Distance:	4-mile loop
Hiking time:	3 hours
Elevation gain:	400 feet
Hikable:	Year-round
Map:	City of Palo Alto

A small lake surrounded by tules and cattails can be found near the north end of 600-acre Arastradero Preserve, and an oak-studded ridge crosses the southern end. Between the two there are more than 6 miles of trails, formerly ranch roads, where it is easy to find peace and solitude. The American Youth Hostel Association is planning to convert a large old house in the southern portion of the preserve into a hostel, and proposed trails will connect the preserve to other parks and preserves in the region.

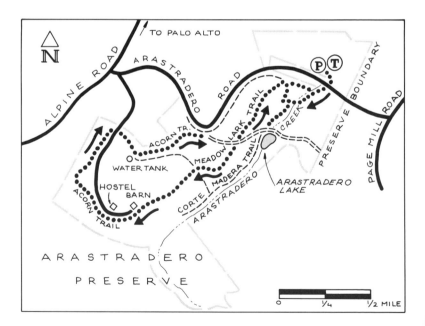

Large, open grasslands of peninsula parks are dotted with solitary oaks.

Take the Page Mill Road exit off I-280. Head south to Arastradero Road and turn right. The preserve parking lot is on the north side of the road in 0.5 mile. Take the path from the parking area across Arastradero Road to the preserve entrance.

The Corte Madera Trail follows along Arastradero Creek from the parking lot to Arastradero Lake. The creek can be a powerful, roiling stream during winter rains, but by summer it becomes a trickle that is an inviting place for children to explore.

In about 0.25 mile the trail crosses over the creek and climbs up a small hill that is covered with orange poppies and blue lupine during the spring bloom. Large oaks rise above the green grassland.

At just past 0.5 mile a gravel road crosses the Corte Madera Trail. Arastradero Lake is another 100 yards or so past the trail junction. You may want to make a visit to the lake, where the children can explore in the reeds and cattails that grow around the shallow edges of this small, tree-shaded lake. Redwing blackbirds and mallard ducks abound here in the spring, and mating noises can be heard from some distance away.

Backtrack to the junction and take the gravel road to your left. In about 0.25 mile the road comes to the Meadowlark Trail. Take a left and begin an uphill climb.

You may see red-tailed hawks or northern harriers as they patrol the grasslands for rodents and other food. Occasionally a great blue heron soars overhead on its way to the lake.

You continue across open grassland that is a carpet of brilliant wildflowers in the spring, and at just over 1 mile Meadowlark Trail crosses the Acorn Trail. Stay on Meadowlark as it continues a gentle climb to the crest of a hill. A beautiful old barn sits on the crest at about 1.5 miles.

Just beyond the barn Meadowlark Trail becomes Acorn Trail, and after you pass through a gate it becomes a gravel road. Straight ahead is the house that is being converted into the Arastradero Youth Hostel.

Acorn Trail leads off to the left of the gravel road, and descends past oak trees that are sprinkled over fields of wild oats that form a green carpet during the spring. Bright wildflowers are visible through the green carpet during the spring and early summer.

At just under 2 miles, near the white boundary fence, Acorn Trail takes a sharp right turn, heads into a forest, and drops down beside a little stream. This is an excellent place to stop for a rest and lunch as the children play around the creek and explore along its banks.

After eating and resting you continue down the trail until it reaches gravel road again at just under 2.5 miles. Cross the road as Acorn Trail takes a right, and go through the opening in the fence as it heads uphill across a pasture.

At the water tank near 2.75 miles you take the trail to the left (both this trail and the one straight ahead are sections of the Acorn Trail) and follow the contour of a tree-shaded hillside. In the cool under the trees, ferns and horsetails grow.

By 3 miles you reach a plateau in the center of the preserve, and the Perimeter Trail leads off to the left. Stay right on Acorn Trail as it crosses a meadow. There are good views of the cities along the shore of the bay from this section of the trail.

At about 3.25 miles Acorn Trail crosses the Meadowlark Trail. Take a left on Meadowlark as it heads gently downhill. Go past the first trail junction until about 3.75 miles, where the Meadowlark Trail dead ends at the Perimeter Trail. Take a right on the Perimeter Trail and return to the parking area.

32. Boardwalk/Catwalk Trails Loop

Type:	Dayhike
Difficulty:	Easy for children
Distance:	1.5-mile loop
Hiking time:	1 hour
Elevation gain:	None
Hikable:	Year-round
Map:	City of Palo Alto

Visit the Lucy Evans Nature Interpretive Center in the Palo Alto Baylands Nature Preserve before beginning this hike. It stands on pilings by a levee on the edge of the marsh and has programs on bay ecology.

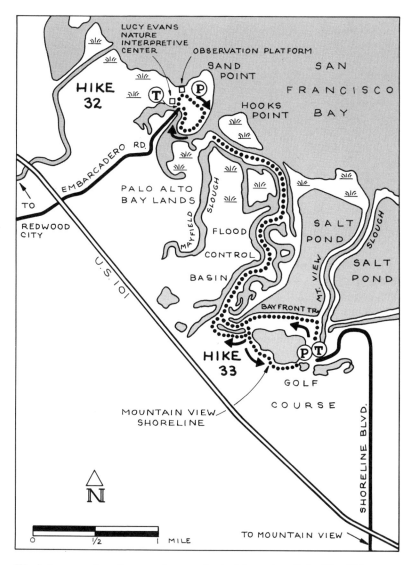

Workshops and walks are also conducted by naturalists. The 120 acres of salt marsh and slough surrounding the center are a wildlife sanctuary, and the trails and boardwalks lead you through samples of several baylands environments.

Take the Embarcadero Road exit off US 101 in Palo Alto and go east for just over 0.5 mile to the sign for the Palo Alto Baylands. Park in the lot to the left at the end of the road.

From the interpretive center, walk across the deck toward the bay

Boardwalks and catwalks take hikers out into tidal marshes.

and follow the boardwalk across the marsh. Some of the many salt-tolerant plants native to these marshes, such as cordgrass, pickleweed, and salt grass, grow beneath the boardwalk, and you get an excellent view of them from above.

 See if you and your children can pick out what "niche" each of these plants live in around the marsh. (Each plant that lives in saltwater marshes has a different tolerance level for salt and for the length of time they can stay submerged under the high tides. Check out your guesses at the interpretive center exhibits.)

Continue straight ahead on the boardwalk until you reach the observation platform at about 0.25 mile. From here you can look out over the mud flats and open water of the bay. Many types of shorebirds can be observed as they seek their food in the shallow water and mud. You may want to bring a bird field guide to help identify these, or you may check out the various local species at the interpretive center.

After watching the shorebirds you can return toward the interpretive center for about 200 yards on the boardwalk until you reach the catwalk that heads south over the marsh. Take a left on the catwalk, which is much narrower than the boardwalk and has no railings. Caution the children that they can get wet and muddy if they fall in here, but there is no real danger since the marsh is so shallow.

The catwalk crosses what appears from a distance to be an unbroken field of cordgrass, but closeup you can see that it is broken by many little streams, sloughs, and mud flats. This is an incredibly rich life zone. Marshes such as this have more living organisms than any other comparably sized plant community in the world. Counting the smallest micro-organisms, there are billions of living things in each handful of mud from the marsh. These small organisms are the bottom of the food chain that extends upward to large shorebirds and small mammals that inhabit marshes.

The catwalk turns to the right as it passes beneath large power transmission lines at about 0.75 mile, and heads overland as it circles the shore of a wide channel where several sloughs join before entering the bay.

There are several benches at the parking area where you can have lunch and look out over the bay and marsh.

33. North Bayfront Trail Loop

Type: Dayhike
Difficulty: Moderate for children
Distance: 3-mile loop
Hiking time: 2 hours
Elevation gain: None
Hikable: Year-round
Map: City of Mountain View

Mountain View opened its Shoreline Park in 1983, and last year more than 1 million people visited there. The 7 miles of paved trails lead hikers and strollers along bayfront and through sloughs and marshes. There are several observation platforms and benches for those who wish to sit and observe. Birdwatchers particularly like these. Much of the park's 544 acres are rolling hills that sit over what was once mountains of sanitary landfill.

Take the Shoreline Boulevard exit off US 101 in Mountain View,

From diving terns to solitary walkers, shoreline parks offer something for all.

eventually head east, and continue 1 mile to the park entrance.

From the parking area, head north along the west side of Mountain View Slough toward the North Bayfront Trail. Depending on the tide, you can watch either shorebirds searching for food in the mud flats, or waterfowl diving for food in the shallow water.

At about 0.25 mile the trail takes a sharp left turn away from the slough and heads west along the edge of a salt pond on the right. This large expanse of water is a Leslie Salt Company's salt-evaporator pond. Water is admitted to this and similar ponds around the bay during the summer when the bay water is at its highest salinity. San Francisco Bay is one of the few places in the country where salt is made by solar evaporation.

The small, brush-covered humps that dot the salt ponds are duck blinds. These have been passed down through family ownership for more than eighty years and are still used during the three months of duck hunting season. They are all at least 500 yards from the shore, far past the range of shotguns, so hikers are not endangered in any way by the hunters.

At about 0.75 mile you can see the levee that borders Charleston Slough to the right, and a trail veers left to circle the forebay of the slough and the freshwater marsh that surrounds it. Information panels along the trail tell you about the many types of birds that feed and nest here. Continue around the forebay until the trail spur returns to the main trail. Take a right on the main trail and walk up the levee on the west side of Charleston Slough.

This levee winds through the slough and its surrounding marshes to a tip of land that juts into the bay between Hooks Point and Sand Point. There, at about 1.5 miles, you are at the bay end of the city's flood-control basin. Birdwatching is excellent along this stretch of the trail. Large egrets use their long legs to carry them through the shallow waters and oozy mud as they search for small animal snacks, avocets sweep low over the marshes as they search for a landing spot, and land birds such as meadowlarks, redwing blackbirds, sparrows, and burrowing owls use the dry land found on the small, low islands in the marsh to feed and nest. The burrowing owl is a reclusive bird that burrows into the ground to build its nest, and children like to hunt for the openings to these. During early evening you can sometimes spot the owls leaving their nests to forage for food.

This point at the end of Mayfield Slough is a good place to stop for a rest or lunch while the children keep an eye out for the many birds, and maybe an occasional muskrat or field mouse. With luck they may even see a marsh hawk dive for food.

Turn around at the point and return by the same route to the forebay. There you can take the trail to the right or the left at the golf course lake. They both wind around the lake and take you to the parking area.

34. Sunnyvale Baylands Levee Trail Loop

Type: Dayhike
Difficulty: Moderate for children
Distance: 4-mile loop
Hiking time: 3 hours
Elevation gain: None
Hikable: Year-round
Map: City of Sunnyvale

The trail here reaches far into the marshes around Guadalupe Slough and loops around the Santa Clara City water treatment ponds. The marshes and ponds provide prime feeding and breeding grounds for dozens of species of waterfowl and shorebirds. As a result, this hike is great for birdwatchers, both beginning and advanced. One distraction for birdwatchers is that at times there seems to be as many runners on the levees as there are birds in the ponds.

Take the Lawrence Expressway exit off CA-237 to Caribbean Drive. After about 1 mile, turn right off Caribbean Drive onto Borregas Avenue. After a short block, turn left on Carl Road and park at the trailhead at the end of Carl Road.

Follow the signs to the levee trail from the parking lot and turn right around the aeration ponds along a saltwater channel. The water in the

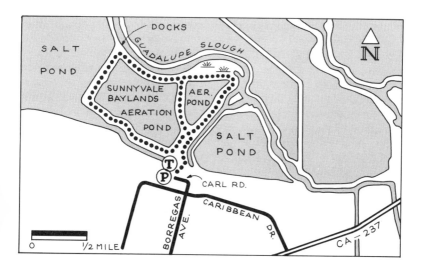

Tidal ponds offer easy access to views of waterfowl.

aeration ponds undergoes tertiary treatment (which removes all ammonia from the water, chlorinates it to kill any remaining organisms, and then dechlorinates it) after it has aerated for 30 days, before it is released into the slough. This makes it safe to the marine life in the bay.

Stay to your right around the aeration ponds as one trail leads off to the left at about 0.5 mile. At about 1 mile the trail takes a sharp left, and on your right are several large salt-evaporator ponds.

Continue straight ahead as the trail follows the north side of the ponds, which have become home to large numbers of waterbirds. The ponds are the largest bodies of freshwater or brackish water in the South Bay, and birds collect there by the thousands.

At just under 2 miles a trail leads off to the left. If any in the party are getting tired, you can take this to return to the parking area for a round trip of about 2.75 miles.

Those who wish to continue will pass close by an oxbow bend of Guadalupe Slough on the right. Great blue herons, coots, willets, pintail ducks, and other waterbirds are plentiful there, and benches have been placed along the trail at regular intervals so birdwatchers can stop and have a comfortable place to sit as they look out over the slough.

The trail continues to follow closely along the slough, which gets deeper and is navigable as the docks for Moffett Field attest, until about 3 miles, when it takes a sharp left turn. The tides along the south end of the bay average about 5 feet, and this area is a good one to watch tidal movements. Have the children guess where the tide is in its cycle, and then see if you can determine whether it is going in or out.

As you take the sharp turn back toward the shore, the buildings of Moffett Field and the Ames Research Station wind tunnels stand out against the dark background of the Santa Cruz Mountains. As you complete the turn, you can see a large hill of refuse near the shore. When this reaches 80 feet in height, it will be reclaimed as a park that offers excellent views over the South Bay.

Continue on the trail as it rounds the aeration ponds and returns to your starting point.

35. Meadow Trail

Type: Dayhike
Difficulty: Easy for children
Distance: 1 mile round trip
Hiking time: 1.5 hours
Elevation gain: 500 feet
Hikable: Year-round
Map: Midpeninsula Regional Open Space District

The Rancho San Antonio Open Space Preserve has several parts, and the 880-acre Duveneck Windmill Pasture section lies at the base of Black Mountain. More than 6 miles of trails wind through bay and oak wood-

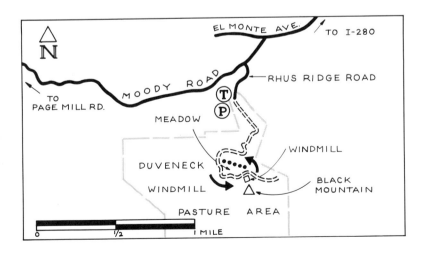

lands and across grassy meadows before ascending the steep slopes of Black Mountain.

Take the El Monte exit off I-280 and head west. Turn left on Moody Road, which is just past Foothill College. After 0.5 mile, turn left on Rhus Ridge Road, and continue for about 0.25 mile. Take a right turn down to the small parking area at the trail entrance.

An old road leads up a wooded canyon from the park entrance. Brightly colored blooms stand out along the trail during the spring, and many varieties of ferns grow along the moist banks.

At just under 0.5 mile, the trail turns around a bend and a meadow appears ahead. From the bend you can see several South Bay cities, but as you move past it, you find yourself in a sheltered meadow that is secluded from any sign of the urban world. Tall oaks border the meadow and Black Mountain rises above it.

The meadow can be enjoyed at leisure as the children attempt to climb the oak trees or look for small animals along the edge of the meadow. After a lunch, return by the same route.

A cool winter's day can be enjoyed by several generations.

36. Deer Hollow Farm Trail Loop

Type: Dayhike
Difficulty: Easy for children
Distance: 2.5-mile loop
Hiking time: 2 hours
Elevation gain: 50 feet
Hikable: Year-round
Map: Midpeninsula Regional Open
Space District

A Santa Clara County Park and the Midpeninsula Regional Open Space District's Rancho San Antonio Open Space Preserve join together to form a 1,100-acre foothill park that consists of a wide diversity of plant communities. The valley floor has creeksides shaded by spreading oaks, and trails lead up through dry chaparral to oak/madrone forests. All of these, plus the easy accessibility of the preserve, make this one of the most popular preserves in Santa Clara County.

Take the Foothill Boulevard exit off I-280. Take an immediate right on Cristo Rey Drive on the west side of the freeway and continue 1 mile to the county park entrance. The preserve trails begin from the northwest parking lot.

Take the trail over the bridge to the north side of the parking lot and veer to the right along the creek. At about 0.25 mile you come to

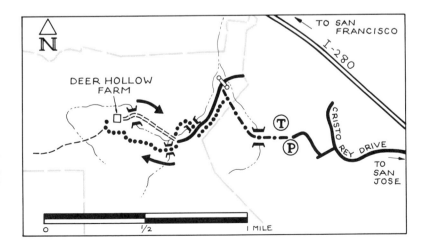

Peninsula parks offer both natural and cultural history to hikers.

an area with unkempt baseball fields and some tennis courts. The creek can be reached through several openings along here, and as you pass the old handball courts, you come to a downed oak that is a favorite climbing spot for children.

Continue on the trail and just past 0.25 mile you come to a gate. Turn left here, and you have a choice of following a paved road or taking a footpath. I prefer the footpath, but if you have a stroller or wheelchair you will want to take the paved road.

The footpath crosses grassland and goes through open oak forests until about 0.5 mile. There it recrosses the paved road and then a foot-bridge across a year-round creek. The children can explore along the banks of the creek in the summer, but it is often a roaring torrent in the winter.

The path follows alongside the road, separated by a picket fence, after it crosses the creek until just before 0.75 mile. There you can either turn to the right to take the road, now dirt, directly to the farm, or you can cross the road, and a footbridge on the left, to head up the side of a hill on the path. This path takes you uphill from the farm around the contour of the hill.

At 1.25 miles you curve back around to enter the farm from the rear.

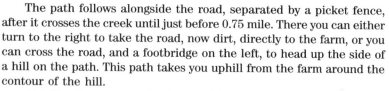

Children like to explore the old farm, operated by the City of Mountain View as a working reminder of the farms that were once common in Santa Clara County.

Return to the parking area by the road or the path.

37. San Andreas Fault/Franciscan/Lost Creek Trails Loop

Type: Dayhike
Difficulty: Moderate for children
Distance: 2.5-mile loop
Hiking time: 2 hours
Elevation gain: 400 feet
Hikable: Year-round
Map: Midpeninsula Regional Open Space District

Los Trancos Open Space Preserve is one of a large number of open space preserves in Santa Clara and San Mateo counties. It contains 274 acres and more than 7 miles of trails, including the 0.6-mile loop of the San Andreas Fault interpretive earthquake trail, which cross over rolling grassland and through cool, shaded forests of oak and bay.

Take the Page Mill Road exit off I-280 and go south for 7 miles. The preserve entrance and a small parking area are located on the north side of the road.

You begin on the San Andreas Fault Trail, which is a self-guided study trail. There are brochures available at the parking lot for this trail, and they are packed with information. This hike does not complete the circle of the study trail, however, but turns left on the Franciscan Trail Loop just before 0.25 mile.

You can look straight up the San Andreas Fault toward Crystal Springs Lake as you cross the meadow on the trail. This fault line marks the junction of two large tectonic plates, the Pacific and the North American, and movement along it causes many of the violent earth movements that have shaken the San Francisco Bay region for centuries.

The trail drops down into a woodland of massive canyon oaks at about 0.5 mile. This trail leading to the woodlands is surrounded by brilliant wildflowers in the spring, and during the fall the deciduous oak and big-leaf maple add color as they turn bright gold and yellow.

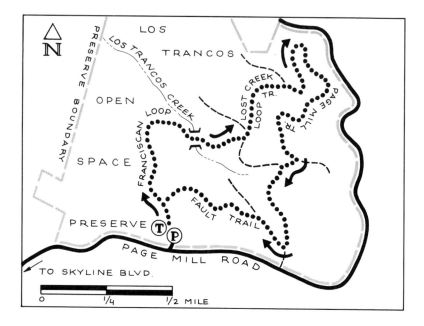

Just past 0.5 mile you cross a bridge over Los Trancos Creek and climb up a short hill to an open area where the Franciscan Trail joins the Lost Creek Trail. Take a left turn and continue up a rise through the woods. At the top of the rise about 100 yards past the junction, and at about 0.75 mile, the trail takes a sharp left and follows a ridge down into the canyon of Los Trancos Creek.

As you descend along the ridge, large fir begin to rise high above the oak, and you can see them across the canyon as you reach the creek. Wild rose and currant add color to the hillsides with their pink blossoms in the spring, and they are joined by the blossoms of false Solomon's seal, star flower, and trillium. Ferns and mosses are thick along the banks and on the boulders of the creek. This is a good place to stop for a rest and to let the children explore along the creek.

At about 1 mile the trail veers away from the narrow gorge of the creek and follows alongside a tributary where tremendous oak and bay shade the hillside. It soon leaves the tributary and begins a climb back to the ridge, joining with Page Mill Trail at about 1.25 miles.

Turn right on Page Mill Trail, and then right again on Lost Creek Trail at about 1.5 miles. This takes you back to the flat and the junction of Lost Creek and Franciscan trails. Take the Franciscan Trail to the left out of the flat as it slowly descends into a group of large bay trees. The trail circles around a small hill and outcroppings of limestone that the children can climb on. Some of the huge oaks in the area have limbs that probably broke off in the violent 1906 earthquake.

The trail climbs gradually into open grassland by about 2 miles. Bright patches of wildflower blooms cover the green hillsides here in the spring.

At about 2.25 miles take the trail to the right. This leads to the San Andreas Fault Trail. At the junction with the San Andreas Fault Trail, take the left fork and head back to the parking area.

Hikes along trails carpeted by fallen leaves are pleasant in the cool days of fall.

Abandoned farm roads make excellent trails.

38. Stevens Creek Nature Trail

Type:	Dayhike
Difficulty:	Difficult for children
Distance:	3-mile loop
Hiking time:	3 hours
Elevation gain:	450 feet
Hikable:	Year-round
Map:	Midpeninsula Regional Open Space District

The various units of Midpeninsula Regional Open Space District and the county park system in this area total more than 4,500 acres. These cover most of Stevens Creek Canyon between Page Mill Road and Saratoga Gap and from Skyline Boulevard to Monte Bello Ridge. This large tract of near-wilderness woodlands, grasslands, and cool, damp canyons where creeks run year-round is located near major population centers on the peninsula. Monte Bello Open Space Preserve, one of the first preserves acquired by the Midpeninsula Regional Open Space District, has almost 2,700 acres and includes the upper reaches of Stevens Creek.

Take the Page Mill Road exit off I-280 and continue 7 miles south on Page Mill Road. Park in the parking lot at the preserve entrance on the south side of the road just past the Los Trancos Open Space Preserve entrance on the opposite side of the road.

From the parking lot take the nature trail straight ahead as it begins a steady descent downhill toward a mixed evergreen forest. The trail

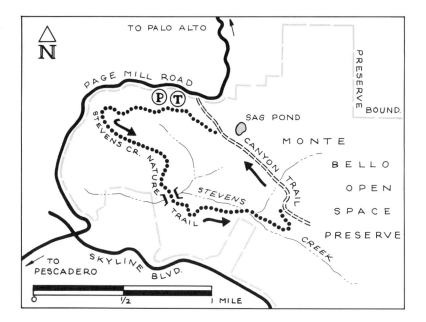

crosses open grassland for the first 0.25 mile, and then takes a sharp left turn into the woods.

Both deer and coyote like the zone where the forest meets the grassland, and you may see signs of them if you look closely. They prefer early morning and late evening for their outings into the open meadows, but you may be able to spot some deer droppings or coyote scat. You may also find some tracks if there has been a recent rain.

From 0.25 mile to 0.5 mile the self-guided trail leads by dead trees that are teeming with life such as woodpeckers, termites, bark beetles, and fungi of various kinds. Just past 0.5 mile there is an area where the hillside slid during the 1983 storms, and the steep scarp where the sliding earth carried large trees is unmistakable.

Just before 1 mile the trail crosses a tributary of Stevens Creek by bridge. The often overflowing stream has formed a small flat where it enters Stevens Creek. This is a good place for the children to explore the creekbed. Insects, and birds that feed on them such as flycatchers, are abundant here, and tracks of deer, raccoon, skunk, and even an occasional bobcat can often be found in the mud near the creek.

The trail begins a short climb after it crosses the bridge and veers to the right. During high water you may want to turn around at the bridge and return by the trail you came on, for there are several spots ahead where you must ford the creek. If the creek is low at the bridge there should be no problem ahead, although the trail may be slippery if there has been recent rain.

Between 1 mile and 1.5 miles the trail follows Stevens Creek upstream. You pass by an area with a thick understory of ferns, berries, honeysuckles, and nettles. These crowd along the creekbanks as horsetails and coltsfoot grow in the streambed itself.

At about 1.5 miles the stream has undercut the creekbank and exposed the roots of some large trees. These are likely to fall in the near future as large winter storms bring flood waters. Have the children guess how the large boulders in the stream got there, and use their size to show the strength of the roaring waters of winter. You must ford the creek here because all of the bridges that have been built across the creek have washed out.

As the trail begins a steep climb uphill at 1.5 miles, there are some terraces where ladybugs love to congregate. Thousands of them winter here in dense clusters on grass stems and tree trunks. They stay near water, but above the winter floods. As the weather warms in the spring they become extremely active and mate. The eggs hatch in April when the larvae eat aphids for about three weeks before pupating.

As the trail climbs up the hill, you can see large fir stumps that indicate there was a heavy stand of fir here like the one still standing across the creek. The trail follows along an old skid road made by loggers about 100 years ago when they logged the large firs that once stood on the hillside. Bay, madrone, tanoak, and an understory of hazelnut and ferns share the hillsides with the fir.

The exposed rock on the side of the road cut at between 1.5 and 2 miles is a bluish-gray serpentine. This is California's state rock, and it was formed by compression along the fault lines that run through the mountains.

At about 2.5 miles a creek flows out of the limestone bedrock uphill from the road. If the children examine the rocks, leaves, and twigs along this creek, they will find that they appear to be fossilized. This is because the hard granular limestone that has precipitated out of the stream water as it flows downstream has hardened as it coated all the items in the creek. This precipitation only occurs in the warm water of summer.

As you pass the stream and look downhill, you can see where the fault zone lies below the road. There is an unusual pattern of ridges and valleys that were formed as the San Andreas Fault broke into multiple fault lines here.

Just past 2.5 miles there is a sag pond with heavy growth of tules and cattails around its edges. This shallow pond was formed at a curve in the fault where gradual movement has forced the edges of the fault line apart, forming a sag in the line where water can collect. This sag pond is fed by springs from along Monte Bello Ridge.

Have the children guess why there is so much growth in the pond. Then discuss how plants die, leaving material that decays and forms sediment that gradually fills in the sag. Plants grow in the sediment, and slowly the pond is filled. This gradual replacement is part of the normal progression that occurs in ponds of all types.

The trail takes off to the left about 100 yards past the pond, and heads uphill through open grassland back to the parking area.

39. Hickory Oak Ridge Trail Loop

Type:	Dayhike
Difficulty:	Easy for children
Distance:	2 miles round trip
Hiking time:	1 hour
Elevation gain:	100 feet
Hikable:	Year-round
Map:	Midpeninsula Regional Open Space District

Looking west from Skyline Boulevard, there are spectacular views of Big Basin State Park in Santa Cruz County and of Butano Ridge. The 1,011 acres of Long Ridge Open Space Preserve are located on the slope to the west of Skyline Boulevard, and the 10 miles of trails that traverse the preserve offer plenty of these vistas as they cross grasslands inter-

Widely spread trees stand starkly above green hillsides.

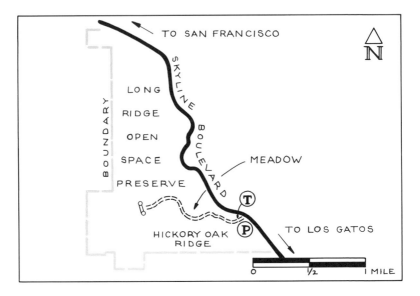

spersed with oak/madrone/Douglas fir forests. Near the southern end of the preserve, Hickory Oak Ridge is home to an excellent hickory oak (also known as canyon oak) forest.

Take Skyline Boulevard south from Page Mill Road for just less than 5 miles (2 miles past the main entrance and parking area for Long Ridge Open Space Preserve) to the small parking area for the Hickory Oak Ridge Area. Park on the west side of the road near the hikers' stile.

Follow the old ranch road as you pass through the hikers' stile, and head through the woods. The road turns right after about 100 yards, and there wide-canopied hickory oaks stand tall over the road. These oaks, also know as canyon or maul oak, have massive trunks, some more than 5 feet in diameter, and their large horizontal limbs are often twisted into grotesque shapes. Have the children look at the limbs and massive trunks and imagine them as characters from some book, maybe "ents" from *The Lord of the Rings* trilogy. The fine-grained hardwood of these trees was used for making farm implements during the 1800s.

At about 0.5 mile, the trail passes out of the trees and into an open meadow rimmed with trees and filled with rock outcroppings. This meadow is full of bright wildflower blooms in the spring, and the view of Oil Creek from the top of the hill is well worth the little side trip.

As you return to the road, you again walk through an oak forest until about 0.75 mile, when you come to open grassland. The road climbs over rolling hills until 1 mile, when you reach a gate that marks the end of the trail.

Return by the same route. You may wish to climb back to the top of the first meadow for a picnic before heading for the parking area.

40. Lookout Trail

Type: Dayhike
Difficulty: Easy for children
Distance: 1.5 miles round trip
Hiking time: 1 hour
Elevation gain: 440 feet
Hikable: Year-round
Map: Santa Clara County Park

Stevens Creek County Park sits among several Midpeninsula Regional Open Space District preserves. It encompasses a large foothill canyon that is site of Stevens Creek Reservoir, and the steep hillsides of the canyon are covered with oak woodlands and open grasslands. Trails lead around the reservoir, along the creek above the reservoir, and to the ridges above the canyon.

Take the Foothill Boulevard exit off I-280 south until it becomes Stevens Canyon Road. About 2 miles from the freeway, the north entrance to the park is on the left. The visitor center and several trailheads are located here. The visitor center is well designed and worth a stop, but the trailhead for this hike is located about 1.5 miles farther along

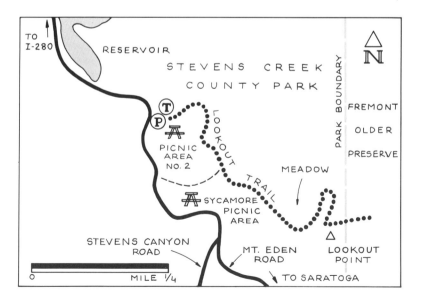

While some wildflowers are tiny spots of color among the tall grasses, others stand out boldly.

on Stevens Canyon Road, which runs through the park, before its inter-section with Mount Eden Road. Take the trail that leads out of Picnic Area No. 2.

The trailhead for Lookout Trail is behind the picnic area rest rooms. It crosses the low ridge that separates Picnic Area No. 2 from the Sycamore Picnic Area, and after about 200 yards a side trail from the Sycamore Picnic Area comes up a small ravine to the right and joins with the Lookout Trail.

Continue straight ahead on the Lookout Trail as it climbs a steep slope. The trail is shaded from the hot, midday sun here as a series of switchbacks leads through an oak and toyon forest. The slopes are an emerald green and wild irises, ferns, and wild roses add color here after the winter rains. During the spring have the children look for small crawling animals among the lush ground growth. They should be able to find several types of caterpillars and many beetles.

The toyon's bright red berries stand out in the fall and winter.

At about 0.5 mile you reach the top of the first ridge. From there you can look south over the Mount Eden Trail.

Continue on uphill to the top of 1,000-foot Lookout Point at 0.75 mile. As you reach the point, continue through the stile that leads out of the county park into the adjoining preserve. From there you have good views of a canyon to the west and the Fremont Older Preserve to the east.

As you return by the same trail, stop along the ridge where you can overlook the meadow below and have lunch. Horseback riders often canter across the rolling hills and trails.

41. Meadow Trail Loop

Type: Dayhike
Difficulty: Moderate for children
Distance: 1-mile loop
Hiking time: 1 hour
Elevation gain: 360 feet
Hikable: Year-round
Map: Midpeninsula Regional Open
Space District

Picchetti Ranch Area Monte Bello Open Space Preserve features a turn-of-the-century winery and farm in its 372 acres. This farm was operated by the Picchetti family for more than seventy years, and is now

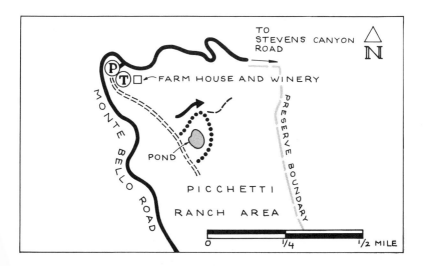

leased by a private party and operates as the Sunrise Winery. Old or-
chards are located near the vineyard, and 2 miles of trails lead through
them to shaded hillsides and open grasslands near a hilltop that overlooks Stevens Creek Reservoir. The old winery and farm are listed on the
National Register of Historic Places and are being restored to their turn-
of-the-century style.

Take the Foothill Boulevard exit off I-280 and head south until Foothill
becomes Stevens Canyon Road. Continue on Stevens Canyon Road about
1 mile past the entrance to Stevens Creek Park. Turn right on Monte
Bello Road and go uphill for 0.5 mile to the ranch.

Manicured areas are often found among wild sections of parks.

Follow the road from the parking lot up past the winery and through the old orchard. As the road begins to curve around the winery, take the Meadow Trail Loop to the right. At just under 0.25 mile the trail, which is still an old farm road, reaches the crest of the ridge from which you can see the pond, and then heads downhill through a thicket of high chaparral. At just over 0.25 mile, take a right as a side trail curves around the pond. This trail takes you around the pond through a small meadow, and at just under 0.5 mile another trail leads off to the right. This completely circles the pond, and rejoins the Meadow Trail Loop just to the south of the pond.

Give the children time to explore the spring-fed pond. (See if they can decide where the water to fill the pond comes from.) There are many small birds and animals that can be seen in the reeds that grow in the shallow edges of the pond.

Large oaks offer shade on the grass-covered slopes by the pond, and you can have a picnic in either shade or full sun.

Return to the parking area by the main trail.

---

42. Seven Springs Trail Loop

Type: Dayhike
Difficulty: Difficult for children
Distance: 3-mile loop
Hiking time: 2 hours
Elevation gain: 360 feet
Hikable: Year-round
Map: Midpeninsula Regional Open Space District

Fremont Older Open Space Preserve, on the edges of urban development, offers 734 acres and a variety of hiking experiences. Its open hayfields, 900-foot-high Hunter's Point, and Seven Springs Canyon all are popular with hikers, and to the west of the park the oak- and chaparral-covered slopes drop steeply down to Stevens Canyon.

Take the CA-85 exit off I-280 and continue south to Stevens Creek Boulevard. Turn left on Stevens Creek, and then right on Stelling Road. Go 2 miles on Stelling to Prospect Road. Turn right on Prospect and continue for just over 1 mile to the preserve parking area.

Follow the road along the creek out of the parking area. This leads

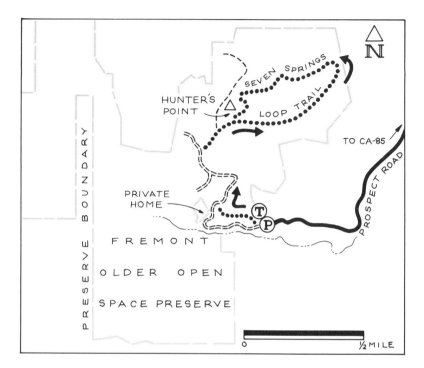

you through an oak and bay forest and at the first bend, at about 100 yards, take the marked hikers' trail off to the right. This trail continues to follow the creek until it dead ends at the ranch road. Take a right on the road and the trail winds uphill with open fields on both sides. In the spring the dark trunks of the old orchard trees stand out against the bright green grass.

At just over 0.5 mile the road reaches a saddle in the ridge and splits. Take the trail to the right. From here the trail follows along the ridge toward Hunter's Point and the Seven Springs area.

Just as you come to the hilltop apricot orchard at about 1 mile where the trail leads off to the left to Hunter's Point, the Seven Springs Trail Loop turns right and heads downhill. There is poison oak on both sides of the old ranch road as it winds down to a lower canyon where many springs seep from the slopes down to the canyon floor.

An old walnut orchard and a clump of bay trees thrive at the bottom of the canyon, and this is an excellent place to stop for a picnic and let the children explore the many holes and knots in the old walnut trees. Many of these holes and crevices are home to insects and small birds, and some of the larger holes even hold enough water for small plants and animals to live in.

At about 1.5 miles the trail reaches the preserve boundary and turns

The profuse, white blossoms of California buckeye stand out against the fresh green background of spring.

north. It then begins to climb up the side of the hill toward Hunter's Point.

At about 1.75 miles you come to a hilltop that is encircled with large oak trees. Just beyond this hilltop is a small apricot orchard. A steep climb of several hundred yards off the trail brings you to Hunter's Point, where you can view all of the Santa Clara Valley.

Return on the road downhill to the parking area.

43. Sanborn/San Andreas Trails Loop

Type: Dayhike
Difficulty: Difficult for children
Distance: 4-mile loop
Hiking time: 3 hours
Elevation gain: 1,200 feet
Hikable: Year-round
Map: Santa Clara County Park

Sanborn-Skyline County Park stretches for nearly 7 miles along the east side of Skyline Ridge from Castle Rock State Park in the southeast north through Lyndon Canyon. In the west there are heavily forested canyons, and numerous year-round streams cut through the ridges to

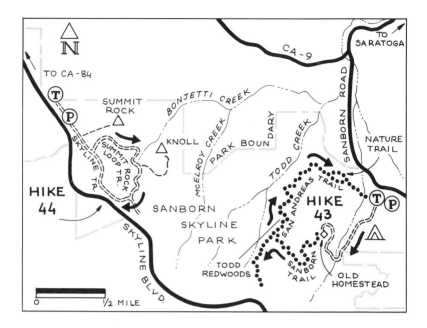

form steep canyons. These steep hillsides weren't suitable for cattle grazing so they were not included in any of the early Spanish land grants. It was only after California became part of the United States that homesteaders from Alpine regions of Europe began to farm the slopes. As the demand for lumber grew, the ridges and canyons were logged of their huge redwoods, but large-scale logging was over in the early part of this century. The 1906 earthquake along the San Andreas Fault, which crosses the park, opened cracks as long as 100 feet and 5 to 6 feet deep as it toppled and split trees. Landslides also left cliffs as high as 40 feet. Only those who are trained observers can see today where this damage occurred, as chaparral and dense forests conceal the destruction.

Take CA-9 west 2 miles from Saratoga to Sanborn Road. Turn left on Sanborn and continue 1 mile to the park entrance.

Take the Sanborn Trail out of the picnic area and head west. The service road takes you through an inviting walk-in campsite near Sanborn Creek. You pass the campground after about 200 yards, and the trail crosses the creek, which roars down into the canyon below after the winter rains. A deer trail leads into the woods as you round a slope into an old clearing. You may get to see a deer going down to the creek if you walk silently as you round the curve.

After about 0.25 mile you return to a forest canopy with fir, madrone, tanoak, and maple all furnishing deep shade for the cool, moisture-loving plants that form the understory.

Just before 0.5 mile you pass an old homestead and can see the grapevines from an old family vineyard through some chaparral growing along the road.

After you pass the homestead, the trail becomes a narrow, steep, rocky climb through thick greasewood and other chaparral plants. Just past 0.5 mile the trail takes a sharp left turn into a canyon where it is shaded by tall firs and tanoaks.

For the next 0.5 mile the trail follows the contour of the canyon on a gentle climb up a ridge. In the summer a cool fog often drifts over the ridge.

At about 1 mile the trail takes you into the canyon, across the creek, and back up the other side into a higher forest. The trail now follows a path through open woods on a soft covering of fallen leaves. At about 1.25 miles the trail appears to fork, but stay to the left for an easier route.

The trail continues to climb to the ridge and rounds it to join the San Andreas Trail at about 1.75 miles.

Stay to the left on the Sanborn Trail as it climbs up a steep slope that is covered with sandstone outcroppings. The slope falls away steeply below the trail, so have your children beware lest they slip and slide for 100 or so feet on an uncomfortable journey.

Tall redwood trees mark the beginning of the Todd Grove. Most of the trees as you reach the headwaters of Todd Creek are only 2 to 3 feet in diameter. These are second-growth trees that grow in circles around much larger stumps that were left after the land was logged in the 1800s.

At about 2 miles the trail reaches a small flat at the headwaters of Todd Creek. Though young trees stand in a thick grove, the area was once

Peninsula trails frequently lead from open grassland into thick stands of oak and bay.

the site of a small grove of trees that had diameters of up to 10 feet.

The creek here was thoroughly disrupted during the logging, and debris left from more than a century ago can still be seen. The ferns and mosses have gradually begun to reclaim the banks for their own, however, as they flourish under the cool, moist shade of the small redwood and fir trees.

This is a good place to stop for a lunch break, and to let the children explore along the banks of the creek. Have them look at the several large redwoods that now grow near the flat and try to imagine what the area was like 150 years ago.

After your break, return on the Sanborn Trail to the junction with the San Andreas Trail. Take the San Andreas Trail as it follows a series of switchbacks down a ridge above Todd Creek. First a grove of madrone carpets the trail with their fallen leaves, and then a stand of fir offers a cool, muted shade.

Near 2.5 miles the trail descends along the east side of Todd Canyon where redwoods cover the hillsides. You continue through this redwood forest with its many rings of young trees that have sprouted from the roots of ancient stumps.

Just past 3.25 miles the trail leaves the redwoods and descends into a flat. As it turns toward the parking area the trail heads along an old road past an old farm site, and then reaches a segment of the self-guided nature trail near the park headquarters.

44. Skyline/Summit Rock Loop/Bonjetti Creek Trails Loop

Type: Dayhike
Difficulty: Easy to moderate for children
Distance: 1.5-mile loop; side trip to knoll, 1.25 miles
Hiking time: 1 to 2 hours
Elevation gain: 400 feet
Hikable: Year-round
Map: Santa Clara County Park

While the previous hike led you high up a ridge to a redwood grove on the east side of Sanborn-Skyline County Park, this one first leads you to the top of a rock outcropping near the west boundary of the park, and

Sculptured rocks offer climbing spots for the children, and photographic scenes for adults.

then down into Bonjetti Creek Canyon. This is one of several wild canyons that can be found on the eastern slope of the Santa Cruz Mountains in Sanborn-Skyline County Park. This cool, deep canyon is an ideal summer hike when the inland areas are reaching temperatures toward 90 degrees.

This trail does not begin on the east side of the park where the main entrance is, but from the western boundary of the park. From the intersection of CA-35 and CA-9, go southeast on CA-35 (Skyline Boulevard) for 1.5 miles to a turnout on the east side of the highway. Park there.

Begin the hike by heading to your right on the old Summit Road inside the park—this is the Skyline Trail. Follow it through a fir, oak, and madrone forest that is typical of those found on many of the ridges in the Santa Cruz Mountains. Muted sunlight filters through the canopy of the tall trees to a pale green growth of ferns and low-growing shrubs such as wild rose and thimbleberry.

At about 0.5 mile a well-worn path leads off to the left to Summit Rock. This large sandstone outcropping only rises about 20 feet above the ridge, but its sloped side drops off quite steeply, and for a surprisingly long way. Children like to climb to the top, and this is quite easy, since there are many holes that have been eroded in the sides. Make sure they are aware of the drop-off, however, if they do climb to the top.

CAUTION

After a side trip to Summit Rock, return to Skyline Trail, turn left, and then take the first trail off to the left. This is the Summit Rock Trail Loop, and it leads down into Bonjetti Creek Canyon. This is one of the many wild canyons that can be found in the Santa Cruz Mountains.

The trail follows an old wagon road across sloping meadows (which are brilliant with wildflower blooms during the spring), and into a fir forest. Some of the older trees here tower above all else and are up to 8 feet in diameter at the base.

At about 1 mile the trail comes out of the forest as it rounds a ridge and enters a slope that leads down to Bonjetti Creek. It passes along a flat where an apple orchard is the only sign left of a long-abandoned homestead. There are also some young redwoods that rise up to 100 feet along here.

You can take a side trip at about 1.25 miles by turning left on a lightly used trail at the sign "To Skyline Trail." The path leads through a corner of the orchard, and then widens into an old road that takes an easy 0.25-mile climb through chaparral to the peak of a 2,800-foot knoll. Oak trees cover the top of the knoll now, but the flat area was probably the site of an old home at one time.

Return to the apple orchard and take a left on the Summit Rock Trail Loop. This section of the trail is cool and shaded, and at about 1.5 miles you climb a narrow ledge between Bonjetti Creek, which cascades over moss-covered rocks at high water, and a waterfall spilling over a large boulder on the other side. During the winter and spring this is an exciting area, and children like the excitement and exhilaration of the sound of water crashing down over the moss-covered rocks. During the summer the flow becomes less forceful, but this gives children an opportunity to explore around the rocks where the water has excavated small ponds.

The trail rejoins the Skyline Trail at about 1.75 miles. Turn right on the Skyline Trail and head north back toward the parking area. The trail crosses a flat ridgetop, where you can hear the sounds of the highway, and through a fir forest before you come to the junction of the Summit Rock Trail Loop at 2 miles.

Return to the parking area by the Skyline Trail.

45. Meadow Trail

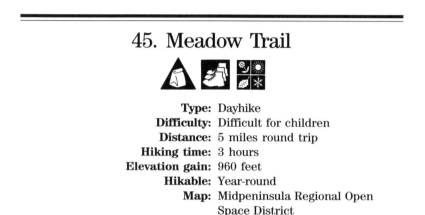

Type:	Dayhike
Difficulty:	Difficult for children
Distance:	5 miles round trip
Hiking time:	3 hours
Elevation gain:	960 feet
Hikable:	Year-round
Map:	Midpeninsula Regional Open Space District

El Sereno Open Space Preserve is named for Mount El Sereno and sits along the 2,500-foot-high ridge where the mountain is located. The 1,036 acres are covered primarily with chaparral, but there are some stands of oak, bay, and tanbark oak in the canyons along the creeks. The

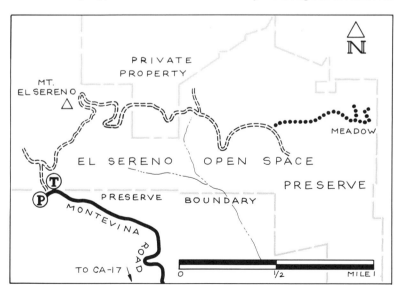

3 miles of trail along the ridge offer panoramic views of Lexington Reservoir, Lyndon Canyon, and most of the South Bay. The exposed trails in the preserve can be extremely hot and dry during the peak of summer, but their well-packed surfaces make them an easy hike even in the dead of a wet winter. Hikers enjoy the warm sun on bright winter days as they walk through the low-lying chaparral.

 Near Lexington Dam on CA-17, turn west on Montevina Road. Continue to the end of the road, and park on the rough shoulder of the road near the preserve entrance.

The trail climbs along the top of a ridge above the steep slopes of Lyndon Canyon, which lies in the San Andreas Fault Zone. On clear days you can see the ocean to the west, and the major landmarks of the South Bay such as the salt ponds along the bay and the peaks of the Diablo Range to the east.

At just under 0.5 mile the trail splits as you head through a group of oak and madrone. Take the right turn as it skirts Mount El Sereno. After several sharp switchbacks you come upon a small, windswept shelf where the benchmarks that mark the elevation are located. This small brass marker set in concrete was placed by the United States Geological Survey when they mapped the region. Discuss with your children how all the land in the United States, or at least almost all of it, has been surveyed at some time by the USGS, and that is how contour maps that show elevations were made.

The trail begins to descend gradually down the side of Trout Creek Canyon. The banks of the creek below are heavily wooded and offer excellent cover for deer. You can generally see one or more of this popular animal foraging on the slopes.

From about 0.75 mile to about 1.25 miles the trail crosses private property. During this stretch please keep to the trail and carefully observe good trail etiquette.

At 2 miles the trail makes a sharp hairpin curve, and the trail splits. Take the opening to the left that leads through the chaparral. After several hundred yards you will leave the ceanothus and scrub oak to enter a sloping grass-covered meadow that is full of bright blossoms in the spring. A number of large oak at the bottom of the meadow have large limbs that swing low to the ground. Children love to play and climb on these, and adults often find a comfortable bend to curl up on for a short nap.

There is a band of bare ground that separates the grass meadow from the surrounding chaparral. For years naturalists thought this was caused by some toxic substance from the chaparral plants, but researchers at Stanford's Jasper Ridge Biological Preserve have discovered that the bareness is the result of overgrazing by small rodents that live beneath the chaparral. They only move a short distance into the meadow for fear of low-flying hawks that can swoop down in an instant to carry them away. If you are at the meadow in early morning or late afternoon, the children may be able to see some of these small animals if they can sit quietly some distance away.

The return hike can be enervating in the heat of the summer, but if you make the hike late in the day for an early supper at the meadow, you can hike back out after the heat has dissipated.

A short rest break is always appreciated.

46. St. Joseph's Hill Trail Loop

Type: Dayhike
Difficulty: Difficult for children
Distance: 3-mile loop
Hiking time: 2 hours
Elevation gain: 600 feet
Hikable: Year-round
Map: Midpeninsula Regional Open
Space District

St. Joseph's Hill, a small grass-covered knoll, is the dominant feature of the small 270-acre St. Joseph's Hill Open Space Preserve. The preserve is located between the town of Los Gatos and the parklands around Lexington Reservoir, and provides a corridor between parks in the northern and southern sections of the Santa Cruz Mountains.

Turn east off CA-17 onto Alma Bridge Road south of Los Gatos. Continue to parking areas on Alma Bridge Road near Lexington Reservoir. Take the gated road uphill from the roadside parking area across from the boat-launching ramp.

The trail is rough and rocky as it heads uphill through a grove of eucalyptus below and chaparral uphill. There are plenty of small birds flitting in and out of the chaparral, especially during nesting season. Even if you don't see any birds, have the children listen closely to see how

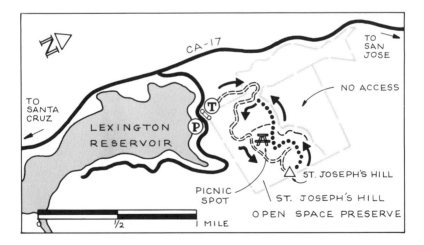

many different bird songs they can pick out as you hike.

At about 0.25 mile the trail begins to drop down into a ravine shaded by bay and oak. This section of the trail crosses a portion of the Lexington Reservoir County Park, and doesn't reach the preserve until just before 0.5 mile.

Just past 0.5 mile a trail leads off to the right. Take this as it begins the climb to St. Joseph's Hill. It follows along an old service road by a cyclone fence. The trail follows the service road around the perimeter of the preserve, but take the first trail that leads off to the right after about 200 yards.

This trail leads around the contour of the hill until another trail leads off to the left at 0.75 mile. If you turn left you come to a bare flat with a single large oak tree about halfway to the top of St. Joseph's Hill. You can take a short rest stop here and have the children guess why the area is level. (Some years ago it was leveled off for a rifle range.)

Animals both large and small can be found in holes like these.

The view opens up out over the bay at the flat spot, but views are much more panoramic from the top of St. Joseph's Hill. If you decide not to make the climb all the way to the top, continue straight ahead on the trail for another 0.25 mile to the service road. Take a left there and head back to the parking area. This makes for about a 2-mile loop.

To continue to the top of St. Joseph's Hill, return to the trail you ascended, and take a left to continue the climb to the top of 1,253-foot St. Joseph's Hill. At about 1 mile the trail takes a sharp turn to the left and drops downhill for about 100 yards before a trail leads to the right. Take the trail to the right and continue straight ahead on it to the top of the hill at 1.5 miles.

The panorama from the peak extends 360 degrees and encompasses San Francisco Bay and the peninsula cities, Mount El Sereno, Mount Umunhum, Lexington Dam, and long stretches of the Santa Cruz Mountains.

On your way down continue around the hill as the trail dead ends. Take a left and then a right as the trail forks at about 1.75 miles. Take a sharp right and head toward the park boundary and some untended vineyards.

At about 2 miles the trail reaches the service road that runs along the cyclone fence at the park boundary. Take a left and follow the service road back to the parking area. From 2 to 2.5 miles the road leads past an old vineyard, and at 2.5 miles rejoins the trail that crosses Lexington Reservoir County Park.

47. Bald Mountain Trail

Type: Dayhike
Difficulty: Moderate for children
Distance: 2.5 miles round trip
Hiking time: 2 hours
Elevation gain: Minimal
Hikable: Year-round
Map: Midpeninsula Regional Open Space District

Sierra Azul Open Space Preserve, at 8,351 acres, is the southernmost preserve in the Midpeninsula Regional Open Space District. It is in reality a collection of three loosely connected preserves that are separated by private holdings. Access is limited in some sections, and others are not

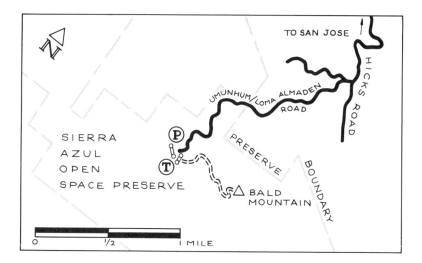

yet open to the public. The Mount Umunhum Area has 2,840 acres, and there is access to the north side. The peak itself is closed to public access, however.

South of San Jose take Hicks Road south past the Guadalupe Reservoir. Turn west on Mount Umunhum/Loma Almaden Road. As you head uphill the road veers sharply to the left. From there it continues past a sign that says "Private Road." There are access rights over this road, but visitors should not venture off it—there is private property on both sides. The gate to the preserve is 2.5 miles from the turnoff south of Guadalupe Reservoir. Park off the road at the gate.

The trail is the fire road that heads east through tall chaparral. This road follows the south slope of a mountain just below its 2,300-foot crest. Downhill from the fire road there are several stands of sycamore trees where springs flow from the hillsides.

To your right the slope falls off quickly into a deep canyon that drains into Herbert Creek up ahead. Several deep, dark canyons can be seen as you hike along this level trail, and the steep slopes above them are all covered with brilliant spots of wildflowers during spring and early summer.

As you head toward Bald Mountain it is impossible to miss one of the highest peaks in the Santa Cruz Mountains, Loma Prieta. This flattened peak is topped by a forest of antennae. The ridge that runs from Loma Prieta to Mount Umunhum, which dominates the skyline on your return trip, is almost as high as the two peaks, and forms a barrier that protects the Santa Clara Valley from powerful incoming storms and winds. The torrential rains from these storms fall on the west side of the mountains, and often cause devastating floods.

e Have the children see if they can tell how the vegetation differs on the east and west slopes of the Santa Cruz Mountains, and determine what may cause that difference.

At about 1.25 miles the trail crosses a saddle in the ridge, and you will frequently be hit by a stiff breeze as you leave the protection of the hills. The trail circles the 2,387-foot peak here, and you can look for a spot where the views are particularly intriguing. Stop for a lunch break and help the children pick out familiar landmarks.

Return by the same trail. On the way back you may want to have the children explore along the boundary of the chaparral growth to see if they can tell what types of plants are included in the chaparral, and what types of climatic conditions are best for this plant community.

Stop and smell the flowers, and notice how they change as spring progresses.

48. Senator Mine/Guadalupe/Mine Hill Trails Loop

Type: Dayhike
Difficulty: Difficult for children
Distance: 4-mile loop
Hiking time: 2.5 hours
Elevation gain: 720 feet
Hikable: Year-round
Map: Santa Clara County Park

The site of Almaden Quicksilver Park along the 6-mile-long Los Capitancillos Ridge was once the most productive quicksilver (mercury) mine in the world. Now 25 miles of trails cross the more than 3,500 acres of the park, where busy mines and 500 homes sat during the heyday of New Almaden. The mines operated from 1845 to 1926, and for a short period again during World War II, and today little remains to be seen of that era. Many of the trails across the park follow the old roads that were used during the mining days. Easy walks and strenuous hikes quickly take hikers away from the hubbub of urban Santa Clara County to secluded woods and panoramic views of the Santa Cruz Mountains.

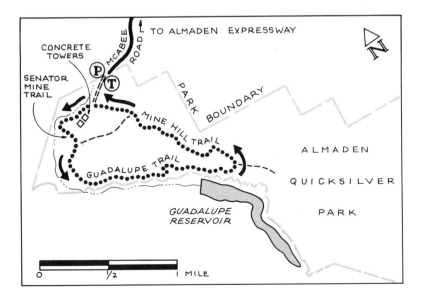

There are three entrances to the park, but for this hike take the Camden Avenue exit off the Almaden Expressway and head southwest to McAbee Road. Turn west on McAbee Road and continue to the end. Park alongside the road.

Rock-strewn creekbeds invite exploration by young and old alike.

Head out on the service road as it follows a creek to the Senator Mine area. The Mine Hill Trail turns to the left after about 200 yards, but continue on the service road, which becomes the Senator Mine Trail.

The canyon widens and you approach two high concrete towers at about 0.5 mile. They were part of the furnace plant, and are left from the days when the mines in the park were producing large amounts of mercury. This mine was worked until the 1920s, and a plaque by the towers tells about the processes they used at the plant to extract mercury from the cinnabar.

The trail climbs along a flat of open grassland and curves up a tree-covered canyon before it ends at a saddle at about 0.75 mile. There it joins the Guadalupe Trail. If you take the left here, you will return to the parking area for a 1.5-mile loop as you follow along a ridge. There are several good picnic spots at the saddle if you want to return to your car after eating.

Take the right if you wish to continue the longer hike, and head downhill toward Guadalupe Creek. Mount Umunhum, at 3,500 feet one of the highest peaks in the Santa Cruz Mountains, can be seen as you head down the trail. This peak is easily identified by the multistoried building on its top. Have the children guess what the building may have been used for. (It was a military installation.)

By 1 mile you can see Guadalupe Creek running below, and the grass-covered hillsides beside the trail have several species of lilies blooming among the high grasses during the spring and early summer.

The trail comes close to the creek by 1.5 miles, but you cannot explore along the banks here because the creek is outside the park boundaries. The meadows here are a brilliant carpet of wildflower blooms in the spring, however, and broad-canopied oak offer intermittent shade as you hike along the park boundary.

By 1.75 miles the trail turns away from the creek and climbs level with Guadalupe Dam, which retains the waters of the Little Guadalupe Reservoir as it stretches 1.5 miles upstream. Although the waters of the reservoir are inviting, the sides of the canyon are so steep that there is little access to the water's edge.

As the trail climbs away from the reservoir at just under 2 miles, there is a place to stop for a rest or a picnic under some oak trees. You can look out over the reservoir as you rest.

At about 2.25 miles the trail turns away from the reservoir and dead ends at the Mine Hill Trail at a saddle. This is a good place to stop for a rest and a picnic if you didn't stop above the reservoir.

Take a left on Mine Hill Trail and head back through open meadows and groves of oak to the park entrance. Wildflowers abound along this stretch of the trail during the spring and early summer. Have the children keep track of how many different types of wildflowers they spot as they walk along the trail.

49. Hidden Springs/Coyote Peak/Ridge Trails Loop

Type: Dayhike
Difficulty: Moderate for children
Distance: 3-mile loop
Hiking time: 2 hours
Elevation gain: 600 feet
Hikable: Year-round
Map: Santa Clara County Park

Coyote Peak, at 1,155 feet, stands sentinel over the 1,600 acres of Santa Teresa Park. A golf course and an archery range occupy much of the low-lying area of the park, and trails crisscross grasslands, rock outcroppings, and forested ravines of the hills around Coyote Peak. The grasslands are a sea of bright-colored wildflowers in the spring, and some bloom even as late as fall as the small, white flowers of tarweed stand out in the brown grasses. There was some mining in the park during the 1800s, but the mines were not very productive. Tailings, or rocks and soil removed from the underground mines, from the Bernal Mine can still be seen on some hillsides.

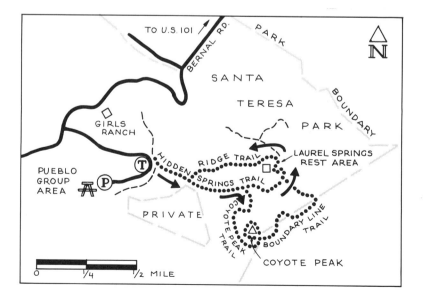

Trails offer opportunities for exercise as well as relaxation.

Take the Bernal Road exit off US 101, and continue south 2.5 miles until you reach the center of the park. Turn left at the first road past the Girl's Ranch, and continue to the picnic area and parking lot.

Take a right turn on the Hidden Springs Trail out of the Pueblo

Group Area. The trail crosses open grasslands that have profuse blooms of wildflowers during the spring and early summer and, as it rounds a hill, crosses a year-round stream at about 0.25 mile.

The Ridge Trail enters from the left, but keep right on the Hidden Springs Trail. Continue uphill past a small, spring-fed pond at about 0.5 mile.

At about 0.75 mile you reach a high saddle, and the Coyote Peak Trail leads off to the right. Take it and head for the top of 1,155-foot Coyote Peak. You reach the peak at about 1.25 miles and, from the level surface that was graded off for a military communications installation during World War II, you have a commanding view of the Santa Clara Valley and mountain ranges to the east, south, and west.

While you are at the peak have the children look overhead to see if they can distinguish the vultures from the red-tailed hawks that are generally soaring above. The vultures have a characteristic V-shape to their wings as they soar, while the red-tailed hawks keep their wings quite level.

You can use either the Boundary Line Trail or the Coyote Peak Trail on your return, but I prefer the Coyote Peak Trail since the other is steep and gravelly. If you do use the Boundary Line Trail, it connects with the Hidden Springs Trail at about 1.5 miles. Turn right and the Laurel Springs Rest Area is beside the trail after about 100 yards.

If you return on the Coyote Peak Trail, take a right at the first junction, and continue on the Coyote Peak Trail as it descends downhill through chaparral and an occasional large tree. At about 1.5 miles the Boundary Line Trail enters from the right. Stay on the Coyote Peak Trail for about 100 yards to the Laurel Springs Rest Area. Turn left into the rest area, where huge old bay trees (also known as laurel trees) form a canopy over picnic tables and a horse-tying rack. A nearby spring feeds a creek that runs all year except in years that are extremely dry, and a luxurious growth of elderberry and fern sprout from this wet area.

Children love to play on the large trunks of several old bay trees that have fallen by the trail. Have them look at the many sprouts that are coming up from both the roots and the trunk. Compare this method of regeneration with that of the redwood, which also sprouts from old stumps and roots.

After a rest stop take the Ridge Trail out of the rest area as it makes a steep climb uphill. At about 1.75 miles it makes several sharp turns, and then begins a series of ups and downs. These take you through open grassland that is full of brilliant blooms during the spring, and under old oaks where there is welcome relief on hot summer days. The Ridge Trail joins the Hidden Springs Trail at about 2 miles. Take a right onto the Hidden Springs Trail, and continue back to the Pueblo Group Area as the trail makes a gentle descent over rolling hills.

Even waterfowl search for shade during hot summer days.

50. Juan Crespi/Pena/Los Cerritos Trails Loop

Type: Dayhike
Difficulty: Moderate for children
Distance: 3.5-mile loop
Hiking time: 2 hours
Elevation gain: 400 feet
Hikable: Year-round
Map: Santa Clara County Park

Rolling hills and oak-studded ridges rise above 349-acre Calero Reservoir in 2,400-acre Calero Park. When the reservoir is full from winter rains (which have been few and far between in the late 1980s and early 1990s), picnicking and boating families flock to this park. When the reservoir is low, as it is at the end of most summers, the parking lots are almost empty and hikers seldom encounter others on the trails. Calero Ridge rises to more than 1,000 feet and runs from the northwest to the southeast in the southern part of the park. Spectacular wildflower displays cover the hillsides in the spring and last until the summer heat withers all exposed objects, including hikers.

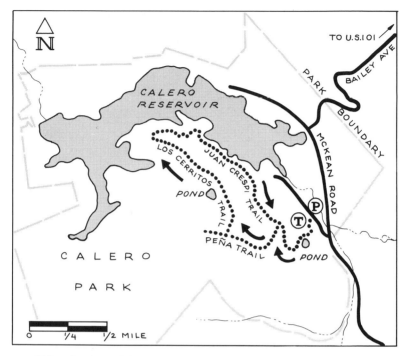

Take the Bernal Road exit off US 101 and head west for 1 mile to Santa Teresa Boulevard. Turn left on Santa Teresa and go 3 miles to Bailey Avenue. Turn right on Bailey. Drive until it dead ends at McKean, and then go left on McKean for 1.5 miles to the entrance to the park on the right side of McKean Road. Park at the picnic area just past the entrance.

Head across the road and turn right on the signed Juan Crespi Trail. It heads on a gentle uphill climb across open grasslands dotted with valley oak that offer cool shade on hot summer days. In the spring these meadows and hills are carpeted with wildflower blooms that stand out against the new green grass.

At about 0.25 mile the trail comes to a low rise, and on the left is a small stock pond that is used by ranchers below. It is also a popular place for great blue herons, who use their long legs to carry them around the shallows of the pond in search of frogs and small fish.

A single oak sits on the west side of the lake, and from there you can often see black-shouldered kites hovering above, on the lookout for rodents scurrying across the meadow.

As the trail passes the dam of the pond, it climbs another small hill and follows an old ranch road as it winds in and out of several small ravines. At about 0.5 mile the Pena Trail leads off to the left. Take it as it begins a steep climb through more open grasslands.

Large valley oak are scattered on the sides of the hills, and these are often home to a variety of birds that can be seen and heard in large numbers during nesting time.

At just past 1 mile the trail veers around a steep canyon and turns toward the ridgetop. The Los Cerritos Trail takes off to the right at a sharp angle just before you reach the ridge. Take this right turn and head down a broad ridge.

Along this section of the trail there are a number of old oak whose limbs droop almost to the ground. Children like to explore beneath these low canopies and look for acorns and signs of the animals that come to eat them.

At a little under 1.5 miles another pond is visible to the left of the trail. The trail continues to descend steadily along the ridge, with an occasional up and down, toward Calero Reservoir. You can see the boat-launching ramp across the reservoir and, on clear days, motorboats and water skiers skimming across the surface of the blue water.

Just before 2 miles the trail widens into a wide service road and becomes the Juan Crespi Trail. It takes a sharp turn to the right, and curves around the east side of the ridge above the lakeshore. The trail winds around coves and inlets, but well above the water, and then leaves the lake as it heads back toward the Pena Trail.

The Pena Trail joins the Juan Crespi Trail at just past 3 miles. Continue straight ahead on the Juan Crespi as it returns past the pond to the picnic area.

51. Swanson Creek Nature Trail Loop

Type: Dayhike
Difficulty: Moderate for children
Distance: 3-mile loop
Hiking time: 2 hours
Elevation gain: 600 feet
Hikable: Year-round
Map: Santa Clara County Park

The drive to Uvas Canyon Park is one of the most colorful in Santa Clara County during the spring wildflower bloom. The trip leads you down backcountry roads through open grasslands and oak woodlands that cover rolling hills. Uvas Creek runs alongside Croy Road on the last leg of the drive, and it is lined with alders, maples, and redwoods the whole way.

The 1,100 acres of the park are typical of the steep, rugged terrain found in the Santa Cruz Mountains, and three live creeks have cut deep canyons as they flow down from Skyline Ridge. The deep canyons are cool, moist, and heavily forested, but the south-facing, sun-drenched slopes are covered with chaparral. The creeks fall in cascades over moss-covered boulders after heavy winter rains, and spring is a favorite time for many to visit the park.

Follow the directions for hike 50 to Calero Park. At Calero Park turn south on McKean Road. This becomes Uvas Road. Continue south past the entrance to Chesbro Reservoir County Park on the left. About 2 miles past the turnoff to Chesbro Reservoir County Park, turn right on Croy Road. Continue on Croy Road to the end and the park entrance. Park at the Black Oak Youth Group Area.

This hike starts along the Swanson Creek Trail as it heads upstream from the picnic area. Have the children decide which way to go after you tell them to head upstream. If they don't know which way is upstream, have them drop a stick or leaf in the stream to see which way it will float. Tell them to take the opposite direction.

At about 0.25 mile you cross to the north side of the creek over a bridge that was rebuilt after a devastating storm in 1986. Have the children imagine how high and strong the flow of the creek must have been to take out a bridge here.

After about 100 yards take the stairway to your left, cross back over the creek, and reach the Nature Trail. This narrow footpath follows closely along the creek. This is a self-guided trail (pamphlets are available from a ranger) that marks native trees and shrubs. Wide-spreading tanoak, maple, and alder provide shade for the trail and the cool-loving plants

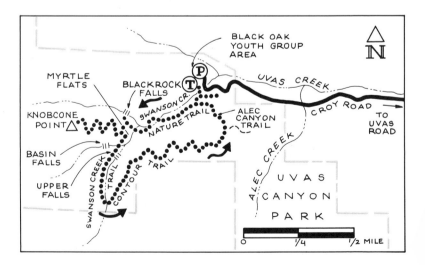

Thistles are pretty, but avoid large stands of them, for they are painful when encountered carelessly.

such as fern and moss that grow on the canyon banks along the creek. This creek often roars as it rushes over the rocky bottom.

The trail crosses over the creek several times before it rejoins the Swanson Creek Trail, as well as several others, at about 0.5 mile. A tributary of Swanson Creek enters at this junction, and a short hike of about 100 yards up the trail straight across from the Nature Trail leads you to Black Rock Falls. There the water cascades over large, dark boulders that give the falls their name. The Myrtle Flats Rest Area is also located at this junction. (Myrtle is another of the many names given to the California bay trees that grow here, as well as another name for the sprawling ground cover also know as periwinkle.)

Return to the junction and take the Swanson Creek Trail left up toward Myrtle Flats. A trail to Knobcone Point leads off to the right here and goes about 0.25 mile up to a hill where a homestead once stood. This is an interesting side trip if your group has energy to spare.

You pass by several signs of former habitation as you head toward Myrtle Flats. Myrtle (or periwinkle), with its bright blue flowers, has covered the hillside, and there is an old cement dam on the creek. A picnic table sits on a terrace above the dam.

At 1 mile there is a wide clearing in the forest, and a spur trail leads off to the right along another tributary of Swanson Creek. Turn up this trail for about 100 yards to Basin Falls, which drops into a small, oval pool among the rocks. Children like to wade and explore here if the falls aren't flowing too powerfully. Have them remove their shoes and socks if they do, for you don't want to have blisters from wet socks.

Return to the main trail and turn right. Almost immediately to the left on the main stream of Swanson Creek is Upper Falls. Just above the falls on the creek there is a large jumble of boulders and fallen trees. Have the children discuss how this jumble may have occurred. (It was left by the violent turbulence of the 1986 floodwaters.)

Walk around the jumble of boulders and logs as the Swanson Creek Trail continues upstream. At about 1.25 miles the trail veers to the left and crosses over the creek. There is no bridge here, so you have to hop across the rocks and boulders and climb the opposite bank.

The trail is called the Contour Trail, and it takes a sharp left turn as it heads out to a broad ridge that climbs gently through an oak forest. There are a number of knobcone pines among the young oak here, which indicates that there was a fire along the slope a number of years ago. Knobcone is one of several types of pine whose seeds sprout only after they have been exposed to the extreme heat of a fire. This, along with the youth of the many oak in the area, supports the idea of a recent fire.

At about 1.5 miles the trail leads down into cool ravines where Douglas fir provide shade for the green understory along several small streams. Gray squirrels, chickaree squirrels, and Steller's jays all can be found here. Most often they can be heard scolding you as intruders into their realm.

At about 2 miles you cross the last ravine along the trail on a wooden bridge built by a troop of Eagle Scouts.

The Contour Trail dead ends into the Alec Canyon Trail at about 2.5 miles. A right turn here takes you on a 0.5-mile side trip to 1,520-foot Manzanita Point and Triple Falls.

A left takes you back to the parking lot at about 3 miles.

---

52. Banks/Blackhawk Canyons Loop

Type:	Dayhike
Difficulty:	Moderate for children
Distance:	2-mile loop
Hiking time:	2 hours
Elevation gain:	420 feet
Hikable:	Year-round
Map:	Santa Clara County Park

Fishing in Sprig Lake, picnicking at a 3,093-acre mountaintop retreat of a nineteenth-century cattle baron, and hiking on 18 miles of trails through the canyons and up the ridges of Mount Madonna Park are all family activities that can be enjoyed here. Mount Madonna rises to 1,897 feet as the high point of the southern Santa Cruz Mountains, and offers panoramic views over Monterey Bay and the plains of the Pajaro and

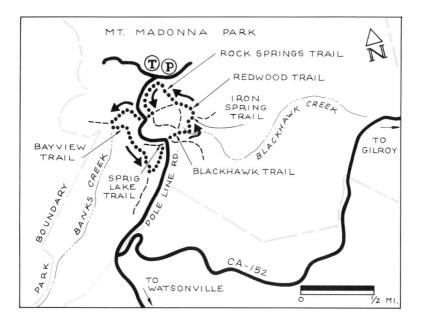

Salinas rivers to the west and the Santa Clara Valley to the east. On exceptionally clear days the Santa Lucia Mountains can be seen to the south and the Diablo Range to the east. Streams roar down the steep canyons in the park over boulders, logs, and whole trees after heavy winter rains. And in the spring the wildflowers stand out brightly against the emerald of the grass-covered hillsides. Both large and small animal life is abundant here year-round.

From CA-152 between Gilroy and Watsonville turn north on Pole Line Road and continue to the park entrance and headquarters.

Head out from the park headquarters west on the service road. After about 200 yards the Blue Springs Trail leads off to the left. Take it and head through a thick growth of chaparral with an occasional knobcone pine rising high above the manzanita and ceanothus. This area has abundant blooms from early spring, when clumps of the manzanita's small, bell-shaped flowers hang from the ends of the stiff branches, through the summer, when yellow bush poppies rise through the brush of the chaparral.

The trail stays east of Pole Line Road as it goes downhill, and at a little less than 0.5 mile you come to the junction of the Blue Springs and Redwood trails. Take a right on the Redwood Trail, which crosses Pole Line Road after about 100 yards, and head downhill on a narrow, shaded footpath. The trail continues a gentle descent toward the head of Banks Canyon through a redwood forest.

Just before 1 mile the trail crosses the head of the canyon and dips down toward a creek. As it passes the creek it rises out of the canyon and joins the Bayview Trail at just past 1 mile. Take a left on Bayview Trail. You get a view of Monterey Bay through an opening in the forest here if the summer fogs haven't come in to hang over the Santa Cruz Mountains. If the fog is in, you are likely to feel drops of condensed fog drip from the limbs of the redwoods as it falls to the ground. Redwoods can gather as much as 10 inches of water a year from fog, and this helps sustain them through the long, dry summers of the California coast.

The Bayview Trail descends down into Banks Canyon and climbs back out on several switchbacks. At just under 1.5 miles Sprig Lake Trail leads off to the right and takes you to a trail junction along Pole Line Road. If you continue straight on Bayview, however, you will have an outstanding view of the Pajaro Valley and the Santa Lucia Mountains.

After another 200 yards take a sharp left turn to head back uphill on a horse trail to the trail junction on Pole Line Road. This junction is at the beginning of Blackhawk Canyon, which is drained by Blackhawk Creek. Three trails lead down Blackhawk Canyon from the junction, and the two left trails lead back to the park headquarters. Take the broad, well-marked Blackhawk Trail as it heads down the east side of the canyon beside the creek. Just after 1.5 miles the Iron Springs Trail leads off to the left. Make the sharp turn, and keep along the slope.

All plants, from the huge redwoods to the small fungi, can be interesting to the searching eye.

Have the children try to guess what causes the rust-colored soil to the left of the trail. (The waters seeping from Iron Springs has vast amounts of iron in it, and some of the iron is deposited in the soil as the water seeps through.)

The Iron Springs Trail joins the Redwood Trail in about 200 yards. Take a sharp left turn onto the Redwood Trail as it heads uphill, and after another 200 yards take a right on the Rock Springs Trail, which leads you back to the park headquarters. If the office is open you can see exhibits of Mount Madonna's natural history.

---

53. Madrone Springs Trail to Lion Spring

Type: Dayhike
Difficulty: Easy for children
Distance: 1.5 miles round trip
Hiking time: 1 hour
Elevation gain: 340 feet
Hikable: Year-round
Map: California State Park

Henry W. Coe State Park is the largest mountain park in the South Bay, with more than 67,000 acres of ridges, deep canyons, and upland meadows and 175 miles of trails. The elevations in the park range from sea level to more than 3,500 feet, and large parts of the park have been classified as wilderness. Almost every ecological zone found in the Coast Range can be found in the park. Oak woodlands, grasslands, coniferous forests, and riparian plant communities are typical here. Spring wild-flower displays are found throughout the park, and are exceptional on Pine Ridge, in Miller Field, and in many of the remote wilderness areas. The giant manzanita found on the western ridges in the park are an unusual plant species, and the stands of ponderosa pine found in several sections of the park are very unusual in the Coast Range. Mountain lions and bobcats are seldom seen, but are known to inhabit the park's wilder regions. Wild pigs are abundant, as well as deer, fox, rabbit, and squirrel, and golden eagle can often be seen soaring above it all. Some of the largest blue schist blocks found in California are located in the south-eastern section of the park. Since the schist is more resistant to erosion than the surrounding sedimentary material, blocks as much as 0.5 mile

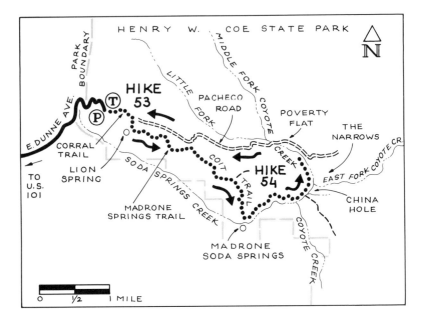

across stand out prominently on hillsides and slopes. These are known as "knockers." There is also a well-preserved marine sediment layer with tiny marine fossils, near the park headquarters.

Take the East Dunne Avenue exit off US 101 near Morgan Hill and go 13 miles to the park entrance.

Take the trail downhill near the cattle-loading chute across from the visitor center. The trail heads downhill behind the barn, and there are signs for Frog Lake and Manzanita Point. Take the Corral Trail toward Manzanita Point for 0.5 mile. The trail parallels a service road along this section of the trail as it passes through open grassland with large black oaks. These oaks have large dark-green leaves with deep lobes and sharp points that turn yellow with a tinge of red in the fall.

The trail follows the gentle contour of the hillsides through these scattered oaks, and then comes to a large flat area. The Corral Trail becomes the Madrone Springs Trail here, and heads off to the right. To the left is the Fish Trail. Take the Madrone Springs Trail to the right as it passes through a forest of digger and ponderosa pine, with some scattered oaks.

Within 100 yards, the trail enters another clearing. Stay on the trail for about 50 feet into the clearing, and then look for a little-used trail to the right. This trail leads you off the main trail to the Lion Spring campsite. The chemical toilet at the campsite also serves as an indicator of the camp location if you can't locate the trail. The campsite is a good spot for a picnic if no one is camped there.

Children like to explore around the outcropping of large boulders near the campsite, and Lion Spring is located behind it. The spring was originally developed as a source of water for ranch cattle, and children who lived on the ranch spent hot summer afternoons at the cool site. Supposedly they sometimes saw a mountain lion atop the boulders above the spring, but few hikers are lucky enough to see this elusive inhabitant of the park today.

Return to the Madrone Springs Trail. If you want to take a longer hike, turn to your right and head east on this trail to visit some of the 100 or more springs that are located in the park. Otherwise take a left and return to the Fish Trail junction. Stay to the left to return on the Corral Trail.

It is exciting to happen upon a broad expanse of emerald green grass broken by a patch of blue or yellow flowers.

54. Madrone Springs/Mile Trails Loop

Type: Dayhike
Difficulty: Difficult for children
Distance: 5-mile loop
Hiking time: 4 hours
Elevation gain: 1,160 feet
Hikable: Year-round
Map: California State Park

There are many long, strenuous hikes along the more than 145 miles of trails in Henry W. Coe State Park, and this one takes you into some of the springs that once attracted Native Americans as well as early settlers because they supposedly had special healing properties. A hotel and resort was built at the present site of the Madrone Soda Springs backpack camp in 1879 and was used until the 1940s. Few remains of the old resort are now visible. Creeks, some that make the trail impassable during the high waters of winter and spring in wet years, form the route for more than 2 miles of the hike, and streamside vegetation offers delightful shade during the hot summer months.

Follow directions for hike 53.

This trail is sometimes impassable during the high waters of winter and early spring. Check with a ranger if you think that the water may be high.

The Madrone Springs Trail heads downhill to the right from the road at the parking lot. Follow the directions for hike 53 as the trail goes across the south face of a grass-covered slope where bright wildflower displays grow during the spring and early summer. Occasional clumps of oak stand on the slopes, and these offer the only shade along this section of the trail.

More than a dozen switchbacks crisscross the ridge as the trail descends down toward Soda Springs Creek.

At about 0.75 mile you pass the trail spur that leads to Lion Spring Camp which is the destination for hike 53. Stay to the right as the Madrone Springs Trail joins with the Coit Trail, and at about 1.75 miles another spur leads off to the right to the Blue Oak Horse Camp. Both of these camps are good rest stops.

At just under 2 miles the trail passes by the Manzanita Point Group Camp, and joins with the Mile Trail, which leads off to the right down to Soda Springs Creek. At just past 2.25 miles the trail comes to the Madrone Soda Springs Camp on the banks of Soda Springs Creek. The large, flat site across the creek was once populated by a large Native

Vistas from East Bay hills stretch as far as the eye can see.

American village, and later by a health resort and hunting lodge.

This is a good spot to stop for lunch and to let the children play around the creek. Have them pretend to be early settlers in the region as they climb around the creek and the stands of madrone trees. You can tell them some tales about how life was in the days when the Native Americans lived here, and later when the Europeans invaded the region.

After you have explored the area at Madrone Soda Springs, cross back over the creek and turn right toward the confluence of Soda Spring and Coyote creeks. The trail leads through a narrow canyon as it crosses back and forth across the creek a number of times. This is an excellent summer hike as the trail stays in the shade of bay and big-leaf maples near the water. Shade-loving plants abound here.

At about 2.5 miles there is an old, abandoned cabin that was built out over the creek. Although the children should not play around the cabin, they can imagine what it may have been like living in it as the creek roared downstream during winter storms.

The creeks come together at about 3 miles as the trail leaves the narrow canyon of Soda Springs Creek. Turn to your left and head upstream on the west side of Coyote Creek. At about 3.25 miles you come to China Hole, with deep pools and rocky beaches, where you can stop for a swim on hot summer days. China Hole Camp is on the opposite side of the creek.

After you take a wade or a swim, continue upstream for about 50 yards until you come to the junction of the Middle and East forks of Coyote Creek. You can see up the steep canyon of the East fork, which is named "The Narrows."

Continue straight ahead on the Middle fork of the creek toward Poverty Flat. You may have to wade along here, or at least do some rock hopping, so prepare to have your children either change shoes or be ready to take out dry ones when you get through this section.

At about 3.75 miles the creek comes to the Pacheco Route, which was the main ranch road in the area before the park was developed. Climb out over large boulders to the road, and you are at Poverty Flat.

This large flat now is the site for a backpack camp, but it was once home to one of the largest Native American settlements in the region with its excellent water supply, good fishing and hunting, and plenty of fruit and berries in the forests.

After you have the children explore around the flat for signs of either Native American or European homesteaders, return to the parking lot on the Pacheco Route for 1.25 miles.

55. San Felipe/Barn/Hotel Trails Loop

Type:	Dayhike
Difficulty:	Easy for children
Distance:	2-mile loop
Hiking time:	1 hour
Elevation gain:	120 feet
Hikable:	Year-round
Map:	Santa Clara County Park

At 9,000 acres Joseph D. Grant Park is the largest Santa Clara County park, and it sits in the Diablo Range with high wooded ridges and sheltered valleys. The park headquarters is in an old ranch house, which also contains a museum of the region's wildlife. There are more than 40 miles of trails in the park, and they range from short walks around the headquarters to long, strenuous hikes to the high ridges. The trails are for the most part old ranch roads, and are broad and well kept. Most follow gentle

Take time to explore solitary oak trees such as this one as you hike through the parks.

grades, and some are used extensively by equestrians and bicyclists.

Take the Alum Rock Avenue exit off I-680 and go east about 2 miles to Mount Hamilton Road. Turn right on Mount Hamilton Road and go 8 miles to the park entrance. Park by the visitor center.

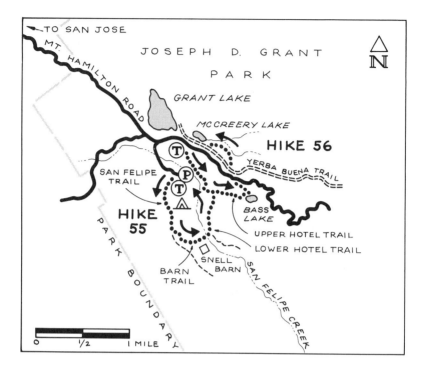

Head out from the parking lot west toward the old barn and corral. Turn south (left) at the old corrals to the trailhead for the San Felipe Trail. This trail follows the road to the family camping area at about 0.25 mile. The campground is located to the left of the trail in a grove of trees.

As you pass the campground the trail enters a small, grassy depression that has several oaks scattered over it. This meadow is an emerald island during the spring, and is carpeted with splotches of blue, yellow, orange, and white flowers.

Continue on the San Felipe Trail to the Barn Trail, which takes off to the left at just past 0.75 mile. The Barn Trail passes by the large, white Snell Barn that was built in the 1800s, but still is in use by the park for hay storage.

The Barn Trail gently drops down to the valley toward the Hotel Trail. San Felipe Creek crosses the trail at about 1 mile. This crossing can be muddy during wet weather, but at other times the children may want to explore along the wet edges of the creek to hunt for frogs and other small water creatures. At about 1.25 mile the Barn Trail dead ends at the Lower Hotel Trail. Turn left here, and follow along the edge of the valley until you reach the Upper Hotel Trail at about 1.5 miles.

Turn left on the Upper Hotel Trail and return to the parking area.

56. Lake Loop

Type: Dayhike
Difficulty: Moderate for children
Distance: 3-mile loop
Hiking time: 2 hours
Elevation gain: 340 feet
Hikable: Year-round
Map: Santa Clara County Park

Joseph D. Grant Park has 40-acre Grant Lake and two smaller lakes (Bass and McCreery) where hikers can fish for stocked trout and bass. There is a large marshy area around Grant Lake that has been set aside for an environmental study that is explained in the museum. The fields around all the lakes feature delightful wildflower displays every spring as blossoms can be seen in the sunny meadows, under the cool shade of oaks and buckeyes, and on the damp slopes of the steep ravines.

Follow the directions to hike 55.

Take the Upper Hotel Trail to the right from the park headquarters as it climbs uphill. At about 0.25 mile a path heads uphill to the left across a grassy slope. Follow it as it climbs beside a small stream, and you reach Bass Lake at about 0.75 mile. This reservoir is stocked with fish, and children may wish to try their luck fishing. If not, they can explore around the shallow edges of the reservoir with the hopes of finding some frogs or watching dragonflies flit through the reeds and cattails.

There is a picnic table under the wide canopy of an old oak near the lake, and adults can sit there as the children play at the water's edge. They can also walk in the meadow at the south end of the lake where wildflowers form a colorful carpet during the spring.

As you leave Bass Lake, take the trail to the west as it makes a steep climb to Mount Hamilton Road at about 1 mile. The trail turns left just before the road. Head downhill until you reach the hikers' stile. Cross the road here to the stile on the other side, where a path heads downhill into the ravine that leads to McCreery Lake.

Take a right on the Yerba Buena Trail (a wide fire road), however, and go around several bends until the rolling pastures open to present a brilliant display of wildflowers during the late spring. Return to the path leading downhill after you make this 0.5-mile side trip.

The path follows alongside a stream as it heads for McCreery Lake,

If you walk quietly you may come upon a family of California quail.

and it soon leaves the open grassland to enter the shade of an oak and buckeye forest. The creek's banks are covered with wildflowers in the spring, and most of the flowers found in the park grow along this stretch of trail.

At about 2 miles the small creek enters a larger one, and the ravine opens up into a sheltered meadow. McCreery Lake is at about 2.25 miles. The lake is popular with both fishermen, who catch plenty of bass, and picnickers, who like to laze beneath the sycamore trees or wade in the shallow waters along the edge of the lake. Children like to hunt for small water animals and look for bird nests in the reeds and cattails.

After a stop, take the trail from the northwestern end of the lake as it heads downhill to Mount Hamilton Road. There is a stile across the road that takes you to the Upper Hotel Trail. Return to the park headquarters.

57. North Rim Trail to Eagle Rock

Type: Dayhike
Difficulty: Moderate for children
Distance: 2.25-mile loop
Hiking time: 2 hours
Elevation gain: 340 feet
Hikable: Year-round
Map: Santa Clara County Park

The land for Alum Rock Park was first acquired in 1872, and the canyon of Penitencia Creek has been a popular outing for families since then. The name for the park, which was known simply as "The Reservation" for years, comes from a huge 625-foot-high rock that stands on the north side of the canyon where the park's entrance roads join. Alum Rock and the taller Eagle Rock nearby are both of volcanic origin, and have withstood erosion as surrounding sedimentary material has been washed away. After World War II the park was overrun by visitors with their cars, and fragile plant communities were almost destroyed as steep hillsides and unstable soils eroded from overuse. Since then parking has been limited to control the number of visitors, and Penitencia Creek remains a charming creek that flows over large boulders through a shady canyon. More than 13 miles of trails wind through the 700 acres of the park, and one, Creek Trail, is designated as a National Recreation Trail.

Take Alum Rock exit off I-680 and continue east to the park entrance. Continue to the parking lot at the end of the road in the park.

The North Rim Trail leads out of the upstream end of the parking lot as it heads uphill. After about 100 yards a service road that is closed to hikers leads off to the right, and the North Rim Trail to the left. Stay to the left as the trail continues a gentle climb above the canyon below.

At about 0.5 mile you reach a level area with several large buckeye trees that provide shade for a short rest. Have the children look for the buckeye seed. This is the largest seed produced by any tree in North America. The whole pod is one seed.

At the flat area the Trail Loop leads off to the right uphill. Take this short loop as it reaches a high ledge near the park boundary at about

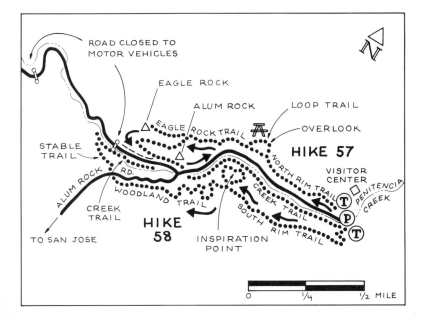

Groups can enjoy picnics after hiking along the trails.

0.75 mile. The views are excellent from here as the ledge overlooks the Santa Clara Valley. Have the children pick out familiar landmarks.

Continue on the Trail Loop until it rejoins the North Rim Trail at about 1 mile. There are several picnic tables at the junction where you can take a refreshment break. Have the children guess how the old palm trees on the hillside above came to be there. (There was an old ranch site and house there.)

Continue on the North Rim Trail to a fork at about 1.25 miles. Take the right fork on the Eagle Rock Trail to a steep climb to Eagle Rock, where you can see across the Santa Clara Valley to the Santa Cruz Mountains to the west, at least on a clear day.

Return to the fork in the trail, and take a sharp right turn as the North Rim Trail heads downhill below Eagle Rock. The upthrust of rock on the downhill side of the trail here is volcanic in origin, and hikers should stay off the crumbly material.

At the junction near 1.5 miles, take a left and then another left after about 200 yards. You are now on the Creek Trail, which will take you upstream as it passes just below Alum Rock, and then crosses the park road at about 1.75 miles. The old bridge here was built for the Alum Rock Steam Railroad in the 1800s. The railroad once went through a tunnel on the south side of the bridge, and a plaque on the crumbled rock tells the story of the old railroad.

The Creek Trail takes you back to the parking lot as it winds along the creekbanks that are shaded by tall sycamore trees and colored by wildflowers in the spring and early summer. As you walk along the trail you can talk to your children about what a train trip along the creek in the late 1800s may have been like.

---

58. South Rim/Woodland/Creek Trails Loop

Type:	Dayhike
Difficulty:	Moderate for children
Distance:	2.5-mile loop
Hiking time:	2 hours
Elevation gain:	400 feet
Hikable:	April to October
Map:	Santa Clara County Park

This hike is only accessible during the summer months; the portable bridge is removed so that it will not be damaged during heavy winter rains. The main feature of this hike is the interpretive overlook where the geologic origins of the region are explained. A branch of the Calaveras Fault cuts under Alum Rock Park, and both volcanic and seismic activity have been important in the development of the landforms in the park.

Follow directions for hike 57, but park by the visitor center.

A spur of the South Rim Trail begins just upstream from the visitor center. Turn right on this spur as it heads abruptly up the steep canyon wall on the south side of the creek. After about 200 yards the trail levels off and turns west before it joins the main South Rim Trail at about 0.25 mile. Bear right on the South Rim Trail and continue west. At just under

0.5 mile you cross the paved bike trail, and then take the trail that leads off to the right.

At just under 0.75 mile you come to the overlook at Inspiration Point. A log fence keeps hikers away from the sharp drop-off at the point, and wooden benches that sit under the shade of young oak trees offer excellent views of the park. A plaque near the overlook describes the canyon's origins, which were volcanic and seismic, and tells about the branch of the Calaveras Fault that cuts underneath the park. Penitencia Creek follows the fault line, and you can follow its tree-lined path as it runs through the canyon.

After you have read the plaque with your children have them look out over the canyon to see if they can spot evidence of volcanic and seismic activity. For volcanic activity look for large outcroppings of volcanic rock, and for seismic activity look for the Calaveras Fault. If you can't

Volcanic rocks stand above the floor of Alum Rock Park.

spot the fault itself have the children look at the creek, and ask why it might be the route of the fault line. (The depression formed by the fault line provided an easy route for the creek to follow as it drains out of the canyon.)

You can see Eagle Rock as it rises 795 feet (more than 300 feet above the creek level) on the opposite side of the canyon. Below it are a number of ledges that were formed by earthquakes in previous centuries.

Return to the main trail by either of the spurs that lead from the point. Where they rejoin the main trail take a right turn and you are on the Woodland Trail.

Continue west on the Woodland Trail as it crosses over the park road at just under 1 mile and then becomes the Stable Trail. Continue past the trail that leads to the left down to the stables as you switch back and forth downhill.

At about 1.5 miles you come to the Creek Trail. Take a right and head upstream. There are several places where you can ford the creek, but stay on the south side until you come to the portable bridge that crosses the creek at the Eagle Rock Picnic Area at about 1.75 miles.

The trail winds in and out of parking areas and picnic sites until it crosses the road at the Rustic Landing Picnic Area. Continue until the trail makes several sharp switchbacks and joins the North Rim Trail at about 2 miles. Take a right on the North Rim Trail as it crosses the old railroad bridge and joins the Creek Trail. Follow the Creek Trail back to the visitor center.

59. Los Coches Ridge Trails

Type: Dayhike
Difficulty: Difficult for children
Distance: 2 to 4 miles round trip
Hiking time: 1 to 2 hours
Elevation gain: 200 feet
Hikable: Year-round
Map: Santa Clara County Park

Ed R. Levin Park centers around a 2-mile-long valley that is surrounded by ridges that reach to 2,500-foot Monument Peak. Most of the activity in the park is focused in the valley where there are lakes, ponds, and large grassy meadows. The park is also popular with equestrians and there are rental stables and parking for horse trailers. Crowds fish for blue gill, crappie, and bass on the weekends, and picnickers watch hang gliders soar from several launching sites. The trails on Los Coches Ridge take you away from the crowds, however, and they offer pleasant walks year-round, even during the hot summer months. The east side of the ridge offers plenty of shade, and breezes cool hikers on the ridges and hilltops.

Take the Calaveras Road exit off I-680 and follow Calaveras Road for 4 miles east to the park entrance.

This trail system winds through the oaks on the east slope of Los Coches Ridge until it circles the high point of the ridge at 740 feet. The distance you hike depends upon your choice of trails once you reach the ridge area.

Begin the hike from the main parking lot at park headquarters. Follow the Spring Valley Trail to the left as it passes the Oak Knoll Group Area. The Los Coches Ridge trails begin after you cross the Vista Ridge Road at about 100 yards.

A small canyon marks the head of the trail system, and you turn right there to follow a trail along the side of the hill. The hills on the east side of the park come into view as you climb slowly up the hillside.

At about 0.25 mile two trails join from the left. Take a left here on either and head uphill toward the open ridge. This is a popular equestrian ride, and the trails are so narrow that you must observe proper trail etiquette. Stand quietly to one side and let all horses pass without making

sudden movements. Emphasize the reason for this to your children so no one gets injured.

As you reach the ridge there are fantastic vistas of the San Francisco Bay Area that include Mount Tamalpais to the north, the Santa Cruz Mountains to the west, and Monument Peak to the east.

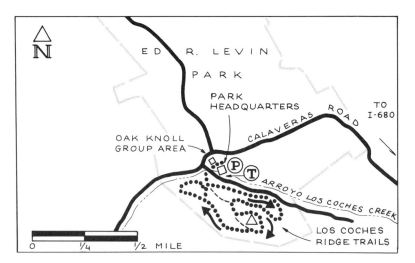

From green, manicured lawns to the undeveloped grasslands that cover park hills, hikers can enjoy hiking in East Bay parks.

Have the children pick out some of the more obvious landmarks of the San Francisco Bay region, such as various mountains, the bay itself, various cities, and even their own neighborhood if you live within sight. If they miss any landmarks that you are familiar with, point them out.

This is also a good hike for seeing soaring hawks and vultures. Have the children try to pick out which of the large birds soaring overhead are hawks and which are vultures. (The hawks soar with their wings almost straight; the vultures soar with theirs in the shape of a large V.) You may even spot a golden eagle if you are lucky. Golden eagles and vultures are both much larger than hawks, but golden eagles' wings are straight, resembling those of hawks, rather than V-shaped, like those of vultures.

At this point you can take any of a number of trails as they wind their way around the knolls at the top of the ridge. Whichever you take will eventually lead you to the top, where you can take a break and look out over the vistas as you eat lunch.

For your return, a good choice is to take the trail on the south side of the knolls as it heads along the boundary of the park through groves of oak. Continue straight on this trail past several trails to the right as it heads toward Spring Creek and Calaveras Road.

As you approach Calaveras Road, the hillsides open up and are brilliant with wildflowers during the spring bloom. A trail leads off to the left, several hundred yards after the trail takes a sharp turn back to the east above Calaveras Road. Take this shaded trail back to the parking lot.

Alameda County

The climb to Mission Peak crosses plenty of open grassland.

60. Hidden Valley/Grove/Mission Peak/ Horse Heaven/Peak Meadow Trails Loop

Type: Dayhike
Difficulty: Difficult for children
Distance: 6-mile loop
Hiking time: 3 hours
Elevation gain: 2,100 feet
Hikable: Year-round
Map: East Bay Regional Park District

The centerpiece of 1,875-acre Mission Peak Regional Preserve is Mission Peak. At 2,517 feet it is one of the prominent landmarks of the southern portion of the San Francisco Bay region, and those who climb to its summit are rewarded with an outstanding panorama of the area. From the peak hikers can see all of the southern arm of the bay, as well as the peninsula from south of San Jose north to Mount Tamalpais. To the east Mount Diablo, San Ramon Valley, and the Hamilton Range are visible. Although the peak is small even by comparison to such Bay Area peaks as Mount Diablo and Mount Hamilton, it rises so abruptly a half-mile above the plains near Fremont that it grabs your attention. Two

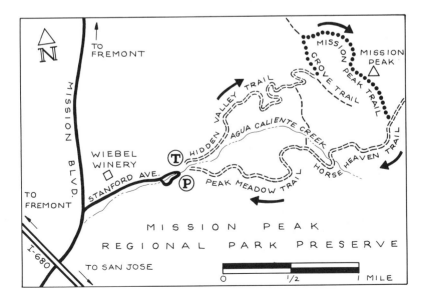

unusual aspects of the climb to the top of Mission Peak are the stone walls that can be found along the ridge on the east slope and the many gliders that soar around the upper slopes.

Take the Mission Boulevard exit off I-680, and head north. In about 0.5 mile turn right on Stanford Avenue and continue to the end of the road at the park entrance.

This long loop is best taken on an overcast day in the summer, or during the cooler days of spring and fall, because the climb is strenuous for most, and very difficult for anyone under ten years or so.

Take the Hidden Valley Trail on the old fire road that leads toward the peak from the parking area. It heads up the west slope of the peak through open grasslands that are bright green in the spring and full of brilliant wildflowers. By midsummer the green has turned to gold as the grasses have dried up and the wildflowers have disappeared.

For the first 0.25 mile the trail follows close by a creek that is a pleasant place to explore during the winter and spring, but that often disappears between midsummer and the beginning of the winter rains.

At just past 0.25 mile the trail veers to the left away from the creek and heads into a series of switchbacks as it heads ever upward. Continue on the trail as it passes a trail off to the right at about 1.5 miles. At just past 1.75 miles the Hidden Valley Trail dead ends into the Grove Trail.

Take a left on the Grove Trail, and at about 2 miles it meets the Mission Peak Trail in a saddle along the ridge. Take a sharp right onto the Mission Peak Trail. Here you are about 600 feet below the peak. As you make the steep climb toward the peak you can see the Sierra Nevada in the far distance to the east on a clear day, and closer peaks such as Mount Hamilton, Mount Diablo, and Mount Tamalpais.

As you near the peak you will feel the breeze that blows constantly, and see some of the sailplanes (gliders) that use the thermal uplifts that originate on the slopes of Mission Peak as the ground warms up.

The soil gets thinner and the grasses get shorter as you climb higher up the peak, and near the top the ground is almost bare of cover. Hawks and vultures share the sky overhead with the sailplanes. The planes appear stiff and primitive alongside the graceful flight of the large birds. See if your children can spot any small sparrow hawks as they hover above the meadows in search of small rodents that may scurry out from their underground protection. This jay-sized hawk is one of the few raptors that actually hovers; the black-shouldered kite, which is much larger, is another one that may be seen in the Bay Area.

At about 3 miles you reach the top of Mission Peak, which stands 2,517 feet above the plains below. From there you have one of the best views of the San Francisco Bay Area to be found.

After the strenuous hike to the peak, you may want to take a long rest break as you enjoy the views. As you do, you may have the children search along the ridge that extends off the eastern slope of the peak.

Thick growth covers many East Bay hills and canyons.

There they may find mysterious stone walls that are no more than 2 feet tall. There is plenty of speculation about how these walls came to be, but there is no historical record of them being built. Were they built by early European settlers? Maybe, but the mountain slopes here were never farmed. Were they built by the Native Americans who lived in the region before the Europeans came? Maybe, but they don't seem to follow any tribal boundaries. When you locate the walls, you may want to have your children form their own theories about how they came to be.

As you leave the peak, head generally south on Mission Peak Trail until it crosses the Horse Heaven Trail at about 3.25 miles. Take a right onto Horse Heaven Trail and begin the trek back down the southwestern slope of Mission Peak across grass-covered meadows that are carpeted with brilliant splotches of wildflowers during spring and early summer.

At about 4.25 miles the Horse Heaven Trail joins the Peak Meadow Trail. Take a left here and continue downhill 1.75 miles to the parking area.

61. Canyon View Trail to Little Yosemite

Type: Dayhike
Difficulty: Moderate for children
Distance: 3.5-mile loop
Hiking time: 2 hours
Elevation gain: 400 feet
Hikable: Year-round
Map: East Bay Regional Park District

Alameda Creek, the largest stream in the county, winds through the southern part of 5,924-acre Sunol Regional Wilderness, home to a large array of wildlife, including even an occasional mountain lion and bobcat. The creek offers excellent birding, with 30 to 40 species, including the brightly colored yellow-billed magpie, seen along it often in a single morning. Great boulders of serpentine and schist indicate a turbulent geological past, as do the massive basalt outcroppings at Indian Joe Cave Rocks. There are also sandstone outcroppings with marine fossils that indicate the region was once under water. This hike takes you into the region known as "Little Yosemite," a narrow gorge on Alameda Creek with huge boulders and rushing water.

Take the Calaveras Road exit south off I-680, and after about 5 miles turn left on Geary Road. Follow Geary Road to the end, and enter the

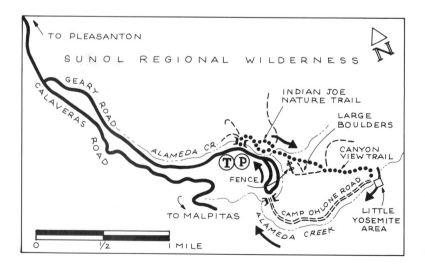

park. Park near the park headquarters before the end of the road.

From the rest rooms and parking area near the park headquarters, cross Alameda Creek on the large metal footbridge and turn right on the Canyon View Trail. This trail leads along the north bank of the creek, and after about 200 yards you can go down to the creek from the trail. The children will like to explore here, but let them know that there will be other places to play along the creek farther along on the trail.

The Indian Joe Nature Trail leads off to the left on the opposite side of the trail. You may take this side trip and return to the Canyon View Trail at about 0.25 mile, or you may continue along the bank of the creek until the trail begins to head uphill at 0.25 mile.

The climb here is moderately taxing as the trail leads up the side of a steep ravine. At about 0.5 mile the trail forks. Take the right, and continue up the steep section of the trail. Several hundred yards past the fork, the trail levels out and veers to the left. To your right you can see a lightly used trail that leads along a fence to some huge boulders in the midst of a small grove of oak trees. Take the lightly used trail to the right.

The moss-covered boulders are a favorite climbing spot for children, as are those about 220 yards farther uphill. The McCorkle Trail crosses the meadow here as it heads uphill to join the Canyon View Trail at just under 0.75 mile. Take it to the junction, and then take a right on the Canyon View Trail as it leads around the contour of a steep slope. This section of the trail is shaded by an occasional oak, and the hillsides are covered with bright wildflowers in the spring and early summer.

At about 1.25 miles the trail crosses a saddle and begins a slow descent down the other side of the ridge. From here you can see the canyon that has been cut by Alameda Creek. Just before 1.5 miles you

Close examination of individual grasses shows the beauty of the seed heads.

reach a trail junction. Take a sharp right here as a spur of the Canyon View Trail leads down to Alameda Creek and the Little Yosemite area. You reach the creek and the large granite boulders that give the area its name just past 1.5 miles. This is a good rest stop and lunch break, for the children will like to explore along the banks of the creek and climb on the large boulders.

After heavy winter rains the creek roars over the large boulders and the children should not attempt to climb out onto them. The water level falls fairly quickly after the rains subside, and the children can explore the creek and boulders safely.

From the Little Yosemite area take a right on the Camp Ohlone Road as it follows Alameda Creek back toward the park headquarters. The East Bay Water District requests that you not wade or swim in the creek because it is part of the city water supply.

At about 2.75 miles the road crosses Alameda Creek on a large bridge with a hikers' stile. From here you can follow the paved road to your right, or you can hike along Alameda Creek back to the parking area.

---

62. Boardwalk/Muskrat Trails Loop

Type:	Dayhike
Difficulty:	Easy for children
Distance:	1.5-mile loop
Hiking time:	1 hour
Elevation gain:	Level
Hikable:	Year-round
Map:	East Bay Regional Park District

Coyote Hills Regional Park is a 966-acre wildlife sanctuary that includes grass-covered hills, freshwater marshes, fallow fields, and willow runs. Each of these provides habitats for a variety of birds and mammals throughout the year. It is during the winter and migration times, though, that thousands of birds can be seen in the park as they come there to feed and rest. Trails and a boardwalk lead visitors through all the major habitat areas in the park and up into the rocky miniature mountain range known as the Coyote Hills. When de Anza's exploration party first looked out from the East Bay hills they saw the surrounding marshes as they were flooded at high tide, and mistakenly thought the hills were islands that stood up from the southern end of the bay.

Take the Paseo Padre Parkway exit off CA-84 (Nimitz Freeway) and

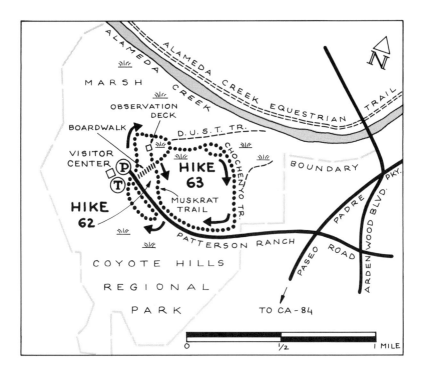

go north 1.5 miles to Patterson Ranch Road. Turn west on Patterson Ranch Road, and continue 1 mile to the visitor center.

Cross the road from the visitor center to the beginning of the boardwalk. This walk takes you over a freshwater marsh that is full of life. The boardwalk follows a winding course as it crosses small ponds, through reeds and cattails that are above the heads of the children, and over large open bodies of water. Have the children look for large flying insects such as dragonflies and for various waterbirds that feed in the nourishing marshes.

Several benches are located along the 0.25 mile boardwalk, and these make excellent observation points for birdwatchers.

The boardwalk ends at the Muskrat Trail. You can take a short side trip by turning left and heading along the trail into the marsh for about 200 yards. From the observation deck there you can watch the wide variety of waterfowl and shorebirds that feed in the marsh. This is especially exciting during the fall migration and the spring breeding periods.

Return to the junction of the boardwalk and Muskrat Trail and head straight on Muskrat Trail as it leads you across the higher and drier portions of the marsh. During the rainy season this trail can be flooded as the marsh becomes a large, shallow lake, so check with the visitor

Ducks, boardwalks, and ponds attract young children.

center to make sure you can cross it on your hike without getting your feet soaked.

New growth springs forth along the trail after the winter lake has dried up, and many birds come to feed on the plants and small insects that become active then. If you don't have binoculars of your own for watching the birds, you can rent them at the visitor center.

Have the children observe the vast quantities of cattails and reeds, and discuss with them how the Native Americans used this almost inexhaustible supply of material for food and shelter.

At about 1.25 miles the Muskrat Trail crosses the road, passes a trail that leads off to the right, and then turns sharply to the right as it heads back toward the visitor center.

---

63. Chochenyo Trail

Type: Dayhike
Difficulty: Moderate for children
Distance: 3-mile loop
Hiking time: 2 hours
Elevation gain: Level
Hikable: Year-round
Map: East Bay Regional Park District

The area where Coyote Hills Regional Park is located was inhabited by Native Americans for more than 2,200 years before Europeans first explored the San Francisco Bay region. There are four Indian shell mounds that span that 2,200 years within the park. Shell mounds are actually the accumulation of debris and other material that remains at the sites. In other words, they are the garbage piles of people living as long as 2,200 years ago. The mounds became known as shell mounds because shellfish from the bay were the primary food eaten by the Native Americans who lived at the sites.

Follow the directions for hike 62.

Cross the road from the visitor center and veer to the left of the boardwalk to the Chochenyo Trail. The trail heads across the marsh for 0.25 mile and then takes a sharp right turn as it becomes the D.U.S.T. Trail.

The D.U.S.T. Trail heads toward Alameda Creek across the marsh, and this is an excellent birdwatching area, particularly during fall migration and spring breeding times.

Thick stands of tule rushes bisected by boardwalks offer hikers solitude.

At about 0.75 mile a spur trail leads off to the right and jogs as it rejoins the Chochenyo Trail. Take this spur as it crosses the high marsh toward the village site with its mounds.

You reach the village at about 1.5 miles, and the trail leads around both sides of the enclosed site. You can look through the chain link fence at the partially reconstructed site. If you are interested in knowing more about the site than you can learn by observing and reading the plaques, you can make reservations for a ranger-led walk that is held on most Sundays at 2:00 P.M.

If you are on your own, you can have your children explore the site by walking around its perimeter and discussing what life must have been like there. Talk about how long it must have taken for the village residents to have built the midden mound of shells.

From the village site the trail leads generally south through a dry area where you may spot many small animal tracks. If you are there in the late afternoon or early morning you may even see some of the small animals if you are very quiet and observant.

At about 2 miles the trail takes a sharp turn to the right just before it reaches the park road. It then follows along the road until it reaches the Muskrat Trail at about 2.5 miles. You can either cross the road and follow along the other side as it returns to the visitor center, or stay on the same side as it heads to the boardwalk.

64. Tidelands Trail

Type: Dayhike
Difficulty: Easy for children
Distance: 1.25-mile loop
Hiking time: 1 hour
Elevation gain: 150 feet
Hikable: Year-round
Map: San Francisco Bay National Wildlife Refuge

The San Francisco Bay National Wildlife Refuge contains more than 23,000 acres of marshes, mud flats, salt ponds, sloughs, and open water. It is the largest urban refuge in the National Wildlife Refuge system, and hundreds of thousands of birds that travel along the Pacific Flyway visit the refuge each year to rest and feed. Many others live there year-round,

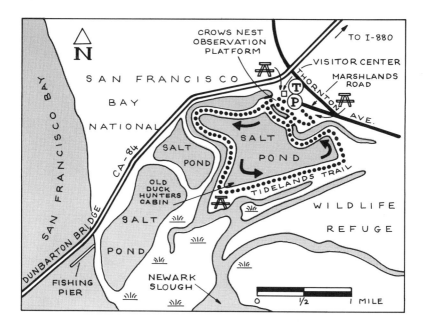

including the rare bay clapper rail. The American avocet is common here, and has been chosen as the refuge's emblem. Stilts, egrets, herons, terns, and many kinds of ducks are found in huge numbers in the refuge. Hikers and birders should always stay on the marked trails, especially during the nesting season. Nesting birds complain vociferously when people get near their nests, and some have been known to dive-bomb intruders.

From CA-84 go south on Thornton Avenue just before the Dumbarton Bridge and follow the signs on Marshlands Road to the visitor center.

From the parking area take the path to the visitor center, where there is plenty of information about the refuge and the bay, and start your hike from the overlook behind the center. Go left and head uphill to the high point of the refuge. From the crow's nest observation platform here, you can look out over Newark Slough and the salt ponds that make up most of the refuge.

There are picnic tables here, so you can have a snack before you head out around the ponds, or you can stop here at the end of your hike.

As the trail leads downhill, it passes by several information panels that explain the history of the region and by an outcropping of chert, a material that was used for arrowheads by Native Americans.

Take the Tidelands Trail as it drops to marsh level and crosses a bridge to the levee. Stay to the right as the trail leads along the levee, with a marsh and tidal slough on your right and a salt-evaporator pond on your left.

A boardwalk leads hikers past an old duck hunter's shack in the marshlands of the San Francisco National Wildlife Refuge.

These ponds were once used by Leslie Salt Company to produce thousands of tons of salt by collecting salt water during the warm summer months and letting the water evaporate, leaving large amounts of salt. Now they are the home to many species of birds that feed on the brine flies and brine shrimp that live in the shallow, salty water.

The trail continues around the edge of the salt pond, and at about 0.75 mile comes to an old duck hunter's cabin at the edge of the slough. The cabin has been left much as it was at the turn of the century, and the story of duck hunting in the area is told on information panels here.

Just past the cabin an old salt company pump house has been converted into a picnic shelter where you can have lunch as you watch the birds in the marsh.

Continue on around the salt pond until you come to another bridge across Newark Slough. Take a right, cross the bridge, and then take either a right or left to return to the visitor center and the picnic tables there.

65. Isherwood Staging Area

Type: Dayhike
Difficulty: Moderate for children
Distance: 4 miles round trip
Hiking time: 2.5 hours
Elevation gain: Level
Hikable: Year-round
Map: East Bay Regional Park District

The Alameda Creek Regional Trail follows the banks of Alameda Creek from the mouth of Niles Canyon west to the San Francisco Bay, a distance of 12 miles. Alameda Creek is home to many birds and small mammals, and it was a valuable source of freshwater for the Ohlone Indians who settled along its banks. (Hike 63 involves a tour of shell mounds left by this tribe.) An early industry along the creek, which continues today, was gravel quarrying. The Alameda Quarries Regional Recreation Area is being developed at the site of twelve flooded gravel pits, and sits alongside the Alameda Creek Regional Trail.

Take the Paseo Padre Parkway exit off I-880, and head east. Park at the Isherwood Staging Area, which is the beginning point for this hike, at the northeast corner of Paseo Padre Parkway and Isherwood Road.

You have the choice of hiking along a paved bicycle trail on the south side of Alameda Creek or along a gravel hiking trail on the north side, as you leave the Isherwood Staging Area east toward Shinn Pond.

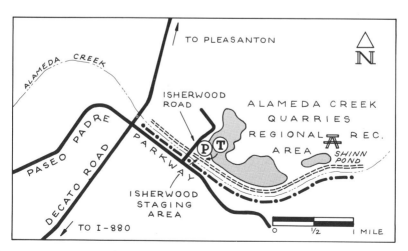

Small flowers often form large clusters of color.

The Alameda Creek Regional Trail passes along a creek that was long ago tamed, channeled, and denuded. As a hiking trail, it has its limitations; as a biking trail, it has many good features. Even as a hiking trail it offers a level, smooth, and sunny hike along a creek that is being resurrected from its cemented state. Waterfowl and small songbirds can be seen along the way, and the area around the Alameda Creek Quarries Regional Recreation Area is at least different.

Alameda Creek deposited large amounts of gravel along its floodplains at the mouth of Niles Canyon for thousands of years before even the first Native Americans reached the region, and a 400-foot-deep pit of gravel was found there by early settlers. Throughout the last half of the 18th century and the first half of the 19th, millions of tons of gravel were removed from this pit.

By the 1960s some of the quarry pits were more than 70 feet deep, and the water that collected in them had to be pumped out. This caused a major environmental problem, though, as large amounts of groundwater was also being pumped out by farmers in the area. As the groundwater level dropped far below the surface, salt water from the bay began to seep into the aquifers in the area.

One step taken by the authorities was to buy the quarries, dam the creek, and fill the pits with freshwater that could percolate back into the aquifers.

Today the pits are managed by the water district, and the East Bay Regional Park District is developing the surrounding lands for recreational purposes.

The 2 miles of trail between the Isherwood Staging Area and Shinn Pond follow along the large ponds formed from the gravel pits, although they are closed to the public, and lead by an otherwordly landscape that was left from the years of gravel mining.

Birds can be viewed along the entire route and there is fishing at Shinn Pond, where you can take a break, eat lunch, and rest before heading back to the Isherwood Staging Area.

You may want cross over the creek to return on the opposite side from which you came.

66. High Ridge/Vista Peak Trails Loop

Type: Dayhike
Difficulty: Moderate for children
Distance: 3.5-mile loop
Hiking time: 3 hours
Elevation gain: 650 feet
Hikable: Year-round
Map: East Bay Regional Park District

The 3,000-plus acres of Garin and Dry Creek Pioneer Regional Parks are former ranchland that was saved from industrial and residential development by the East Bay Regional Park District in the 1980s. The Dry Creek Ranch was traditionally the site where Washington Township residents celebrated May Day and the Fourth of July, and that practice continues today for residents of all of the East Bay. The large developed areas of the park include playing fields for softball, volleyball, horseshoes, etc., and there is plenty of room for free play. There is also an interpretive program and visitor center at the old Garin Barn where visitors can learn about the ranching and farming history of the Hayward area. The 20-mile-long trail system within the two parks offers an excellent opportunity for hikers to quickly leave the crowds behind, though, and takes you to several peaks where there are panoramic views of the East Bay region.

Take the CA-238 exit off I-580. Continue on CA-238, which becomes Mission Boulevard, just past the light at Industrial Parkway. Garin Avenue is the next street on the left. Turn left and go 1 mile to the park entrance.

Many trails have special areas of interest, such as Newt Pond.

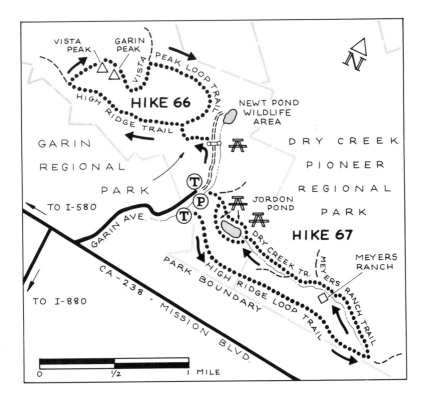

The trail from the parking lot heads up the west side of Dry Creek, which is little more than layers of green algae by late summer. At about 0.25 mile the trail passes through a cattle gate, and a sign indicates that the High Ridge Trail leads off to the left. Before taking that trail, though, continue straight ahead about 100 yards to the Newt Pond Wildlife Area.

Newt Pond and the surrounding marshy area is fed by several year-round springs, and the old ranch road that serves as the trail here often has muddy spots even in midsummer. Children like to explore around the shore of the pond looking for newts, which breed here in the rainy season, and other small water animals. Frogs are plentiful during the summer, but you have to have sharp eyes and be very quiet as you search for them.

Return to the junction with the High Ridge Trail and take a right after you have explored around the pond. This trail climbs steadily as it passes through open grasslands that are brightened by profuse wild-flower blooms during the spring and early summer.

At about 1.5 miles the Vista Peak Trail (some of the signs have Vista

Park if they haven't been changed) heads off to the right. Take this trail as it winds around Vista Peak at about 1.75 miles and on to Garin Peak. Both of these offer excellent views of the surrounding country, and children like to climb to the tops of both. They are also about midway on the hike, so this is a good place to stop for a picnic and a rest break.

After exploring the peaks, continue on the trail as it begins to descend down the slopes on the east side of the peaks. At about 2 miles the Zeile Creek Trail enters from the left, but stay to your right on the Vista Peak Trail as it continues around the contour of the hills. The trail leads through open grasslands, and rejoins the High Ridge Trail at a little over 2.75 miles.

Take a left at the junction of the High Ridge and Vista Peak trails. At just over 3 miles, where the trail veers left to the Newt Pond Wildlife Area, take a right. There are picnic tables in the grove of sycamore trees on the left side of the trail just past the junction. This is a good place to eat lunch before returning to the parking area.

67. High Ridge/Meyers Ranch/Dry Creek Trails Loop

Type: Dayhike
Difficulty: Difficult for children
Distance: 2.25-mile loop
Hiking time: 2 hours
Elevation gain: 500 feet
Hikable: Year-round
Map: East Bay Regional Park District

Dry Creek Pioneer Regional Park is the eastern portion of this dual park, and offers several attractions not found in Garin Regional Park to the west. Jordon Pond is a short hike from the visitor center, and offers fishing opportunities to all comers. This pond sits in the midst of a landscaped area with picnic tables. Largemouth bass, bluegill, and sunfish have become naturally reproducing population in the pond, and channel catfish are planted in the pond once or twice a year. Another feature of the Dry Creek section of the park is the Chabot Fault, an offshoot of the Hayward Fault, which runs beneath the High Ridge Trail near the crest of the ridge.

Follow directions to hike 66.

Old farm ponds offer sanctuary for waterfowl in East Bay parks.

From the parking area, head back toward the park entrance on the entrance road for about 100 yards to the beginning of the High Ridge Trail. Take a left, go through a cattle gate, and head across an open meadow. This area is full of wildflower blooms during the spring and early summer.

At just under 0.5 mile the trail reaches the crest of a low ridge and crosses the Chabot Fault, a branch of the Hayward Fault. The Hayward Fault is located about 1 mile to the west of the park and has been the cause of several major quakes in the past century. The seismic activity in the area makes the unstable, steep slopes of the park less than desirable land for building.

The Meyers Ranch Trail leads off to the left just past the crest, but continue straight on the High Ridge Trail as it follows along the ridge crest.

At just past 1.5 miles the Meyers Ranch Trail again leads off to the left. Take a sharp left here and head back toward the old Meyers Ranch.

If you wish to take a longer hike you can continue on the High Ridge Trail to about 1.75 miles and take the trail to Gossip Rock, where Native Americans met to grind acorns on the sandstone rocks under old bay trees.

If you take the shorter route, the trail leads down the side of the ridge and follows along Dry Creek. It crosses the creek several times on bridges before it reaches the old ranch house (now a park residence). Continue past the house and corral several hundred feet to the Dry Creek Trail, which leads off to the left. The trail leads beside the creek beneath the shade of oak and sycamore trees until it reaches Jordon Pond at about 2 miles.

Jordon Pond is a landscaped area with lawns and picnic tables and is a good place to eat lunch. Children like to explore around the edges of the ponds and watch the waterfowl there as you rest.

After a break at the pond it is just a short walk back to the parking area.

68. Arroyo Trail Loop

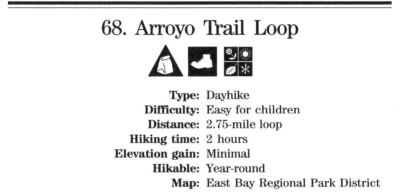

Type: Dayhike
Difficulty: Easy for children
Distance: 2.75-mile loop
Hiking time: 2 hours
Elevation gain: Minimal
Hikable: Year-round
Map: East Bay Regional Park District

The large hole in the ground of Shadow Cliffs Regional Recreation Area was dug by the Sand and Gravel Division of Kaiser Industries between 1930 and 1969. When the quarry played out, Kaiser stopped pumping out the seeping water and donated the land to the East Bay Regional Park District. People come to the recreation area to swim, fish, and birdwatch. Hikers find several short trails, one that leads them around several small ponds to the southwest of the big hole.

Take the Santa Rita Road exit south off I-580. This becomes Main Street in Pleasanton. From Main Street, turn left on Stanley Boulevard. Follow Stanley Boulevard east from town for 1 mile to the park entrance.

From the parking lot, take the Arroyo Trail south toward the levee, and continue straight as it crosses the Levee Trail after about 100 yards. It then loops around a small pond and marshy area where there are many birds and small animals to observe.

The trail returns to a junction at just under 0.5 miles, and you should take a left there on the North Arroyo Trail. The trail follows along the shore of a large lake formed on the slow-moving Arroyo del Valle Creek. There is fishing in this section of the lake, and people catch bass, bluegill, sunfish, and catfish. Birds are also plentiful here, especially during nesting season in the spring.

At about 0.75 mile, halfway along the shore of the lake, a trail leads

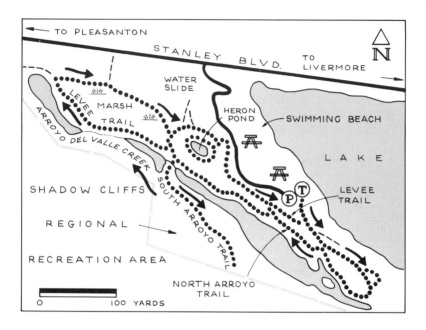

off to the right to Heron Pond. If you wish to make your hike shorter, you can take this trail; otherwise, veer to the left and stay on the North Arroyo Trail as it continues around the shore. At just under 1 mile it dead ends at the South Arroyo Trail.

During the rainy season this trail is inaccessible, but if it is not, you may wish to explore the south side of the lake and the marsh area there. This spur is about 0.5 mile round trip.

After you have taken the side trip, return to the trail junction and continue past it for about 100 yards. A trail heads off to the left to the Levee Trail. Straight ahead is Heron Pond.

Take the left and then another left on the Levee Trail at just over 1.75 miles and head around the marsh. This area is very active with birds and insects during the spring, and you may want to use your binoculars to identify many of the small birds that nest here.

Stay to the right as several trails lead off the main Levee Trail, then take a left as the trail dead ends just before the Heron Pond at about 2 miles. After about 100 yards the trail forks, with the left fork leading to the waterslide area, and the right continuing around Heron Pond.

This is a good place for the children to explore as you take a short rest stop. Frogs and insects are plentiful here, and great blue herons can often be seen hunting the frogs and small fish.

Return to the main trail and turn right. The Heron Pond Trail crosses the Levee Trail to become the North Arroyo Trail at about 2.25 miles. Take a left on the Levee Trail to return to the parking area.

The modern visitor center and observation tower at Hayward Regional Shoreline stand above the surrounding marsh.

69. Marsh Trail Loop

Type:	Dayhike
Difficulty:	Moderate for children
Distance:	4-mile loop
Hiking time:	2 hours
Elevation gain:	Level
Hikable:	Year-round
Map:	East Bay Regional Park District

The 817 acres of Hayward Regional Shoreline was a huge, thriving marshland before the American Salt Company was established in 1865. This company built dikes on the outer edges of the saltwater marshes that were filled with cordgrass to trap saltwater. The dikes formed large ponds of stagnant water that was pumped through a series of evaporation ponds. Salt was then harvested from the ponds. The site was used by the American Salt Company until 1927, when Leslie Salt Company leased the ponds. Since Leslie already operated a large number of ponds in the area, the site was never actively used again. By the 1970s several governmental agencies banded together to purchase the site, and developed a management plan that involved rebuilding the site to its original marshland status. Today the Hayward Regional Shoreline includes the largest restored salt marsh on the West Coast.

Take the West Winton Avenue exit off I-880 and go west to the park entrance.

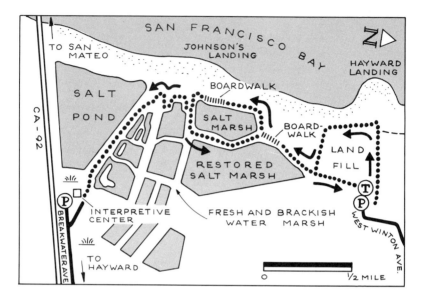

From the parking area take the trail straight toward Hayward Landing as it circles the landfill. After about 0.5 mile the trail takes a sharp left and continues along the shoreline where many shorebirds can be seen, especially during low tide when they feed in the mud flats.

At about 0.75 mile the trail takes another sharp left and then intersects with another trail at a "T" near 1 mile. Take a right at the "T" and head out across the largest restored salt marsh on the West Coast. At just under 1.25 miles you cross a boardwalk, and the trail forks.

Take a right to head toward the bay. The trail bends to the left after about 200 yards and heads toward another boardwalk at about 1.5 miles. This area of the marsh is full of activity as birds flock there to feed on the many small sea animals that live in the life-giving mud of the marsh.

Have the children bend down on the boardwalks to see how many different forms of life they can identify. These may be plants or animals, and some may be very small.

The trail turns to the left about 100 yards past the second boardwalk, and then another trail leads off to the right almost immediately. This trail leads to the interpretive center, where you can learn about life in the marsh and the history of the area.

If you do not wish to take the 1-mile round trip to the interpretive center, continue straight for another 200 yards until the trail turns left and heads back across the restored salt marsh. If you head for the interpretive center, the trail will lead past the edge of a freshwater and brackish marsh. Have the children see if they can tell the difference in the plants that live here as opposed to those that live in the saltwater marsh.

After you have seen the exhibits at the interpretive center, return by the same route until you reach the trail junction at the saltwater marsh. Take a right at the junction to return by a different route that takes you through the center of the marsh.

Have the children look for plants and animals that were described in the exhibits as you make the return trip.

70. Lake Trail Loop

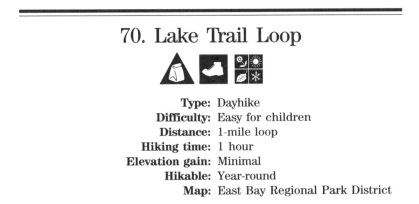

Type: Dayhike
Difficulty: Easy for children
Distance: 1-mile loop
Hiking time: 1 hour
Elevation gain: Minimal
Hikable: Year-round
Map: East Bay Regional Park District

The Alameda County Flood Control and Water Conservation District dammed San Lorenzo Creek in 1964 to form Don Castro Lake. Thousands of tons of dirt and gravel were removed from a nearby hill to fill the dam, and a crater was dug in the flattened area. Today the crater is used as a swimming lagoon and, as part of Don Castro Regional Recreation Area, is one of the most popular swimming spots in the East Bay. While Don Castro Lake is closed to swimming and boating, fishing is allowed. The hike around the lake is short, but surprisingly wild. Turtles and frogs splash into the water as you approach, and ducks nest in the reeds along the edge. Raccoons and deer are often seen near the water in the evening.

Take the Crow Canyon exit off I-580. Take an immediate right onto

Overhanging tree trunks offer shade during hot afternoons.

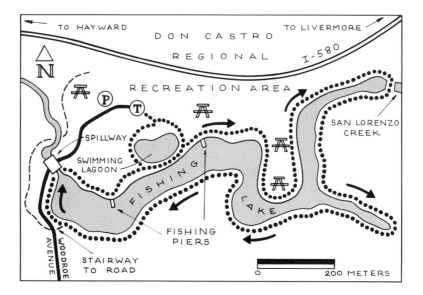

Center Street. Turn left off Center onto Kelley Street at the second stoplight and continue to Woodroe Avenue. Turn left onto Woodroe Avenue and continue to the park entrance.

This short hike around the lake can be free-form. From the parking lot take the Lake Trail as it leads to the swimming lagoon and then head to your left. This takes you past several picnic areas and a fishing pier. Have the children stay close to the edge of the lake, and keep a watch out for turtles that may be sunning themselves on half-submerged logs and an ear for frogs that are croaking among the reeds and cattails.

During the spring there are plenty of birds flitting among the reeds and dragonflies dart about completing their daily tasks.

The trail curves around the edge of a small peninsula after about 100 yards, and then swings back as the lake ends and narrows into San Lorenzo Creek. Keep an eye out for small fish and minnows as you walk along the creek.

At about 0.25 mile the trail turns to cross over the creek on a footbridge, and then follows along the opposite shore on its way around the other side of the lake. About 200 yards past the bridge, the trail turns to the left to circle around a small arm of the lake, where there are plenty of small animals to listen for and to see in the shallow waters.

Continue to explore along the shore of the lake as you head toward the dam, and at about 0.75 mile, just before you reach the dam, there are some stairs that lead away from the shoreline up to the park entrance road. If you take these and cross the road, you come to a trail that leads down below the spillway of the dam and across the creek as it comes out of the lake.

You can also choose to cross the dam and turn toward the swimming lagoon. About 200 yards before the lagoon is another fishing pier. If you want to try your luck for bass, bluegill, and sunfish, this is a good spot.

Both trails lead back to the parking area, and the children may want to take a swim before heading home.

71. Fishing Lake Trail

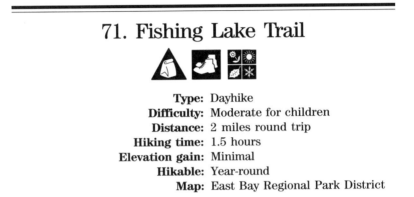

Type:	Dayhike
Difficulty:	Moderate for children
Distance:	2 miles round trip
Hiking time:	1.5 hours
Elevation gain:	Minimal
Hikable:	Year-round
Map:	East Bay Regional Park District

Small 360-acre Cull Canyon Regional Recreation Area is noted for the award-winning complex at its swimming lagoon, but a short hike up Cull Creek, which feeds the reservoir, and around the shores of the lake

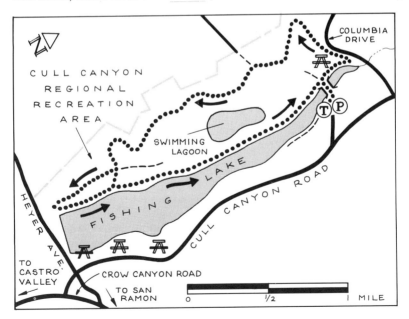

Young hikers enjoy looking for birds and animals in a protected pond.

gives you a good chance to observe the many birds that are found there. Waterfowl can be seen in the lake, long-legged waders along its shores, and tiny birds flitting about in the brush and trees.

 Take the Crow Canyon exit off I-580 and follow Crow Canyon Road to Cull Canyon Road. Turn north on Cull Canyon Road, and then left into the park after about 0.5 mile.

Take the trail north from the parking area to the footbridge. Cross the creek and turn right instead of following the crowds to the most intensely used swimming hole in the Bay Area. The trail follows along the creek for about 100 yards before it takes a sharp left turn just before Columbia Drive.

The trail leads up the hillside overlooking the lake, and after about 200 yards takes a left turn to follow along the contours of the hill. Continue along the contour of the hill past a spur trail off to the right at about 0.5 mile until you pass the swimming lagoon and its fenced picnic area.

Along this section of trail you may see some small birds, and plenty of wildflowers during the spring, as you pass through chaparral and some open grassland.

Past 0.75 mile the trail makes several sharp turns and heads downhill toward the dam end of the lake. Just before 1 mile you come to an intersection. If you continue straight ahead you come to the lakeshore several hundred yards above the dam.

Take a right turn and head down to the dam, and the trailhead. The children may like to explore around the dam, and you can discuss how deep the water is there, and why the dam may have been built. (It was built for flood control and water supply.)

To return take the shoreline trail as it heads back toward the swimming lagoon. Along this stretch of trail the children can look for many different kinds of waterfowl and shorebirds, as well as small animals such as turtles and frogs in the growth along the shore.

At just under 2 miles you return to the footbridge to the parking area. You can either cross the creek here, or stop in the picnic area beside the creek.

72. East Shore Trail

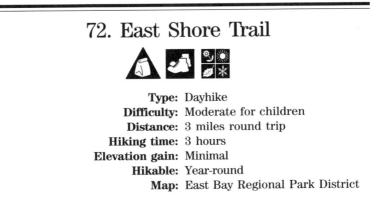

Type:	Dayhike
Difficulty:	Moderate for children
Distance:	3 miles round trip
Hiking time:	3 hours
Elevation gain:	Minimal
Hikable:	Year-round
Map:	East Bay Regional Park District

This 315-acre lake has an intimate feel, with many nooks and crannies along its shoreline that form bays and inlets and an island in the middle. The lake was formed in 1874, when Anthony Chabot, a hydraulic engineer who had worked in the gold country, aimed gigantic water hoses on the hills above San Leandro Creek and washed thousands of tons of debris into the creekbed. He then imported a huge herd of wild horses, which he ran back and forth across the loose debris to pack it into an earthen dam. The lake behind the dam, and the re-vegetating hills above, were off limits to the public from the time the lake was built until the mid-1960s, when legislation was passed that opened the area to the public for controlled recreational uses. Today Lake Chabot Regional Park is one of the most popular fishing spots in the East Bay, and boats and canoes can be rented for trips into the various narrow inlets and bays. Hiking is also a favorite activity here, and most of the trails around the lake are paved, making them accessible to wheelchairs and strollers.

Take the Fairmont Drive exit off I-580, and head east. Fairmont Drive becomes Lake Chabot Road. Continue on Lake Chabot Road to the park entrance.

The East Shore Trail leads from the parking area along the shore of Lake Chabot toward Honker Bay. It leads close to the shore of several small inlets and coves, and past fishing piers that jut out into the lake as it follows the contours of the hill above the shoreline.

At about 0.25 mile you pass Indian Cove, and you get a good view of Live Oak Island offshore. Have the children explore along the shallow waters in the coves and inlets, and look for birds in the chaparral and oaks uphill from the lake, as well as in the cattails and reeds along the shore.

At about 1 mile the trail turns sharply to the right as it comes to Raccoon Point. You may want to walk out to the point and take a rest stop here before continuing on around Honker Bay. You can watch the boat traffic on the lake, and see if you can identify any of the hawks that are soaring above.

Return to the trail and go to your left to continue the hike. If any of the children are tired, this is a good spot to turn around and head

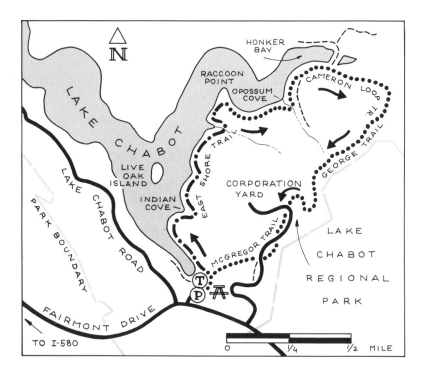

Exposed trails circle most East Bay lakes.

back to the car.

The trail heads through groves of oak that furnish good shade, and a creek comes into the lake at Opossum Cove at 1.25 miles. Another trail leads off to the right just past the cove, but continue along the shore until you come to the bridge across the headwaters of Honker Bay just past 1.5 miles.

As you head across the footbridge you enter into open grassland that is exposed to the southern sun. Here the temperature is appreciably warmer, and it is a good spot to take a break in the winter as the children explore along the shallow waters of the creek as it enters Honker Bay. In the summer they may want to play in the water, but park regulations prohibit any swimming or wading.

To return you may retrace your route along the shoreline, or you may take an alternate route that leads into the hills above the shore. To take this route, take a left turn onto the Cameron Trail Loop as you return across the bridge. Follow this trail around the contour of the hill above the flat valley drained by the creek to just over 2 miles. There the trail joins with the Ten Hills Trail to the left and the George Trail to the right. Turn right onto the George Trail.

At 2.25 miles a trail leads off to the right back to the lake, but continue straight as the trail climbs a gentle grade before making a sharp turn at 2.5 miles. After the turn the trail rounds a hill and comes to a paved road that leads to the county corporation yard. Cross the road and stay on the trail (now McGregor Trail) as it follows along the road and crosses it several times, before a trail leads off to the right at 2.75 miles.

Take this trail back to the parking area.

73. Elmhurst Creek Trail

Type:	Dayhike
Difficulty:	Easy for children
Distance:	3 miles round trip
Hiking time:	2 hours
Elevation gain:	Level
Hikable:	Year-round
Map:	East Bay Regional Park District

The San Leandro Bay Regional Shoreline lies between the Nimitz Freeway and the Oakland Airport. It includes more than 1,200 acres of saltwater marshes, mud flats, open bay, and solid land. You are never isolated from the sights and sounds of the urban environment here, as the sounds of jets taking off or landing compete with those of railroad cars, large trucks, helicopters, and factories. Views are just as urban. The Oakland Coliseum, tall tanks, factory smokestacks, and hillsides scarred by quarries are all visible from any site in the shoreline preserve. These factors notwithstanding, this is a wild place. Small sandpipers can be seen scurrying beneath the stiltlike legs of great blue herons, and thousands of dowitchers, avocets, and other shorebirds invade the mud flats

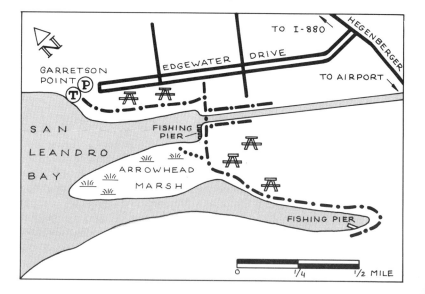

Picnic facilities are found at most regional shorelines.

as the tide ebbs. And this area has been restored to a somewhat wild state since the mid-1970s from a 40-foot-high dump hill called "Mount Trashmore."

Take the Hegenberger Road exit off I-880 and go west to Edgewater Drive. Turn right on Edgewater and continue to the park entrance.

From the parking area take the Elmhurst Creek Trail to the right as it bends around San Leandro Bay. This section of the trail leads past a developed area with picnic tables and an exercise course until it crosses Elmhurst Creek at about 0.5 mile. Just across the creek take a right turn as the trail crosses San Leandro Creek. On your left the San Leandro Creek Trail follows the creek, and on your right are a series of small fishing piers.

At about 0.75 mile the trail enters the Arrowhead Marsh area. On the left is a developed park area with picnic tables and rest rooms, and on the right is a short spur trail that leads out into the marsh. Take this spur to let the children have a chance to put their hands in the soft mud of the marsh to see where the vast amounts of food for the birds and marine animals originates.

Return to the main trail and keep an eye out over the marsh for large birds such as great blue herons and egrets that feed on the small marine animals that live in abundance in the marsh area.

The trail bends around the Airport Channel and comes to an end at 1.5 miles at a fishing pier. Even if you don't fish, this is a good place to take a break and watch the birds that live in the area. Have your children see how many different species of birds they can identify, or at least classify. They don't have to know the names of the individual species, but they can have fun grouping them together, and seeing how many different groups they can see.

Return to the parking area by the same route.

74. Crab Cove to Roemer Bird Sanctuary Trail

Type: Dayhike
Difficulty: Moderate for children
Distance: 4 miles round trip
Hiking time: 3 hours
Elevation gain: Level
Hikable: Year-round
Map: East Bay Regional Park District

This area of the San Francisco Bay shoreline has a long history of recreational use. From the 1870s to the 1930s it featured fancy swimming pools, resort hotels, and Neptune Beach, a large amusement center with a stadium, skating rink, merry-go-round, and other rides. It was often referred to as the Coney Island of the West. The military turned the area into a maritime training center in World War II, and the building that is now used as the Crab Cove visitor center and for naturalists' programs was a military hospital. In 1959 the beach became a state park, and in 1967 the East Bay Regional Park District assumed control. Crown Memorial State Beach is now a very popular park, and people come to it for many activities, especially in warm weather. The marshes, freshwater lagoons, the marine sanctuary at Crab Cove, and a bird sanctuary at the beach are popular for hiking. While the area is very crowded at midday and on the warm days of summer, hikers find solitude here in the early

Families search for treasures along beaches.

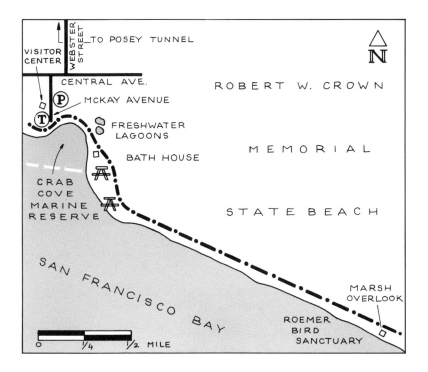

mornings, early evenings, on cloudy, overcast days, and almost any time in the winter.

Take Webster Street through the Posey Tunnel to Alameda. Continue on Webster to Central Avenue and turn right. Go one block on Central and turn left on McKay Avenue. Continue on McKay to the park entrance.

From the parking lot head toward Crab Cove, and turn left on the paved trail as it leads through a developed area with many picnic tables and a bathhouse. Two small freshwater lagoons are on the left just before the bathhouse, and you may want to return to explore them at the end of the hike.

Crab Cove is a marine reserve, and you may not collect any marine animals or plants from the area.

At about 0.5 mile the trail veers to the left as it follows along the top of the beach and heads toward the marsh overlook at the Roemer Bird Sanctuary.

Follow along the path as you keep an eye out for the many shorebirds and water birds that come to the beach to feed, and at 2 miles the marsh overlook is on your right. Take a right and cross the beach to the overlook.

The marsh and the mud flats of the bay around you are part of the Elsie Roemer Bird Sanctuary. This sanctuary is home to dozens of species of shorebirds and water birds, and the overlook is an excellent spot to bring your binoculars and bird guides and spend an hour or so seeing how many species you can identify.

After your stop at the overlook return to the trail and retrace your route to the parking area.

On a warm day your children can swim after changing at the bathhouse, or they can simply wade along the edge of the beach.

75. Redwood Creek Headwaters Trail Loop

Type: Dayhike
Difficulty: Moderate for children
Distance: 2.75-mile loop
Hiking time: 3 hours
Elevation gain: 700 feet
Hikable: Year-round
Map: East Bay Regional Park District

In 1855 a hollow tree stump 33.5 feet in diameter was discovered near Redwood Peak, and the virgin stand of redwoods in what is now Redwood Regional Park may have been one of the most magnificent in the whole redwood region. Two of these magnificent trees were used as markers by sailors as they attempted to miss Blossom Rock near Alcatraz Island. The trees would have been 16 miles from the Golden Gate. This stand of redwoods was logged between 1840 and 1860 as at least ten sawmills operated in the area. Large, raucous shantytowns sprang up around the mills to house the workers. These were violent times in the East Bay, and nature had yet to be tamed. Grizzly bears were known to have prowled by night, occasionally killing cattle, hogs, and horses, and mountain lions often awakened sleeping loggers. Even California condors were said to have flown overhead in groups of as many as fifty—more than exist now. The second-growth redwoods that now stand in the park are more than 100 years old, and offer a cool respite from the busy world of the urban East Bay.

 Take the Redwood Road exit off CA-13 (Warren Freeway), and follow Redwood Road east to Skyline Boulevard. Turn left on Skyline Boulevard and follow it along the crest of the Oakland Hills, veering to the right at the junction of Skyline Boulevard and Joaquin Miller Road. Continue

about 2.5 miles along Skyline Boulevard to the Skyline Gate Staging Area
on the righthand side of the road.

From the Skyline Gate Staging Area take the Stream Trail straight
ahead as it heads downhill past the meadow where the "Girl's Camp,"
a stone hut with rest room and water, is located at 0.5 mile. The trail
follows the upper reaches of Redwood Creek along this section as it
passes through an old eucalyptus grove that has been cleared into a grove
of tall redwoods. These provide shade for the moisture-loving ferns and
trilliums that grow along the hillsides and creek.

At about 0.75 mile the trail begins a short, steep descent to a small
open meadow, and the Eucalyptus Trail leads off to the left. Stay on the
Stream Trail and at 1 mile the Tres Sendas Trail leads off to the right.
Take the Tres Sendas Trail as it crosses the north fork of Redwood Creek
and heads up the south fork. This is a good spot to take a short break
and let the children explore around the banks of the creeks, which are
little more than trickles in mid- to late summer, but which flow strongly
after winter rains. They can search for different kinds of fern along the
creek banks, and turn over old logs to find salamanders and creepy
crawlers.

After about 200 yards take the Star Flower Trail to the left as it heads
up a small ravine. At about 1.25 miles turn right on the French Trail as
it climbs a steep hillside out of a ravine. Continue past the Redwood Peak
Trail as it leads off to the left at just under 1.5 miles, and cross a ravine
that has a thick stand of huckleberries, a cousin of the domestic blue-

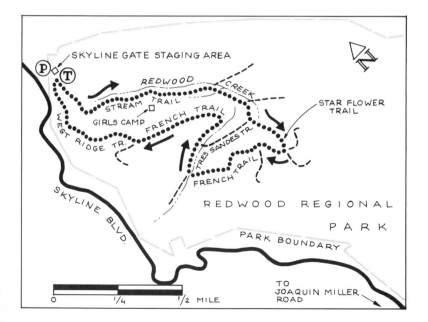

berry. The children can taste this small, blue berry if the birds haven't eaten them all, but make sure they are picking them from the small bushes that look like blueberry bushes.

The trail comes to a ridge, and then drops down into another ravine as it follows a small stream to Redwood Creek's south fork at about 1.75 miles.

Turn right on Tres Sendas Trail at the south fork and go about 100 yards to the junction of the French Trail. Take a left and head up through a thick covering of evergreen broadleaf bay and tanoak. As you reach the ridge just before 2 miles you enter a pine forest.

At 2 miles take a right on the West Ridge Trail to return to the parking area.

76. Huckleberry Path Nature Trail

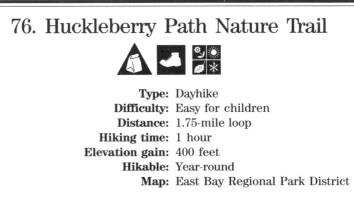

Type: Dayhike
Difficulty: Easy for children
Distance: 1.75-mile loop
Hiking time: 1 hour
Elevation gain: 400 feet
Hikable: Year-round
Map: East Bay Regional Park District

Two small knolls stand sentinel over this delightful ecological relic. Since it is located due east of the Golden Gate, Huckleberry Botanic Regional Preserve receives heavy winter rains and cool summer fogs that provide the moisture needed to support a plant community that is unique

Children like to climb on low-lying limbs such as these.

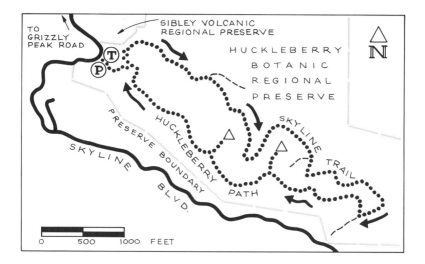

to the East Bay. Brittleleaf and pallid manzanita (which survives in only two places in the world) thrive on the barren, rocky knolls, where they will eventually be replaced by other plants such as huckleberry, silktassel, and chinquapin. This occurs as the leaf litter deposited by the manzanita composts into richer and moister soil. Many of the plants found in the preserve can only be seen in Northern California, some only in the East Bay, and the variety of rare and beautiful plants in the preserve is remarkable for such a small area. In the early 1970s the preserve was threatened by developers, but the fragile preserve and the narrow footpath that leads to it were obtained by the East Bay Regional Park District. Early spring is the most popular time to visit the preserve, and it is often very crowded along the trails in February.

Take the Fish Ranch Road exit off CA-24 just east of the Caldecott Tunnel. At 0.8 mile take a left off Fish Ranch Road onto Grizzly Peak Boulevard and go for 2.5 mile to the intersection of Grizzly Peak Boulevard and Skyline Boulevard. Make another left turn, and go for about 0.5 mile, past the entrance to Sibley Volcanic Regional Preserve, to the park entrance.

Take the trail from the parking area as it leads through batches of blackberries, coyote brush, and poison hemlock. If you don't know what poison hemlock is, you may want to look it up in a field guide so you can readily identify it to your children.

After about 200 yards the trail forks. Take the left fork as it begins a series of switchbacks down the side of a forested canyon toward the Skyline Trail and then climbs out of the Sibley Volcanic Regional Preserve. At just under 0.5 mile the trails join. Stay right and begin a gentle climb around the northern contour of the knolls that dominate the preserve. Broad-crowned bay trees provide excellent shade for the many fern that grow on this northern slope, and there are occasional openings through the canopy that provide views of the Contra Costa hills.

The trail passes a spur to the right at about 0.75 mile. Take this spur if the children are getting tired. It connects with the upper section of the Huckleberry Path and cuts a little more than 0.25 mile off the hike. Turn right as the spur dead ends at the Huckleberry Path. Otherwise continue straight until the Huckleberry Path takes a sharp turn back to the right at about 1 mile as the Skyline Trail continues straight ahead.

Take the Huckleberry Path as it climbs steeply for a short distance before leveling out for its return to the parking area. It is along this upper section of the trail that the most interesting plants in the preserve are found. Have the children find examples of the three different kinds of manzanita that grow along here. You can identify them from the park brochure that is found at the trailhead. Discuss that these plants are found in only a few places and why they should be preserved.

Just before 1.25 miles a spur leads off to the first of the two knolls that rise above the parks. The views from these are excellent, and the rare manzanitas are most abundant here.

Return to the main trail from this 200-yard side trip and turn right to the next spur in about 300 yards.

After making these two side trips, continue back to the parking area.

77. Shore Trail Loop

Type: Dayhike
Difficulty: Easy for children
Distance: 0.75-mile loop
Hiking time: 1 hour
Elevation gain: Minimal
Hikable: Year-round
Map: East Bay Regional Park District

Costanoan Indians who lived along the creek that feeds Lake Temescal used it for bathing and swimming long before the Spanish arrived in the region. The early missionaries named the creek from two Aztec words: tema (to bathe) and cali (house). By 1870 Anthony Chabot had dammed the creek to form 13-acre Lake Temescal, which was used as a source of water for the "tiny" town of Oakland. The 48-acre park that surrounds the lake was one of the three original parks of the East Bay Regional Park District, and was opened as a recreation area in 1936. Today Temescal

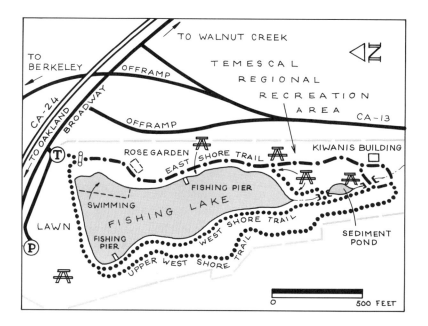

Regional Recreation Area is one of the most popular swimming and hiking spots in the East Bay. It was also the only park in the East Bay Regional Park District that was damaged by the October 1991 fire that devastated so much of the Oakland Hills.

Take the Broadway exit off CA-24 in Oakland. Follow the signs toward CA-13. Park in the lot on the right side of Broadway just before you reach CA-13.

From the parking lot walk to the east shore of the lake to the paved path that leads by the swimming area and rose garden. The Hayward Fault runs beneath the lake just out from the east shore, and the lake sits in a "rift valley" where the fault has long caused sag ponds in depressions. Earth movement is constant, although generally unnoticed, along the fault line, and fault movement evidence is visible at the south end of the lake along the trail.

Follow the trail along the shore of the lake, and at just past 0.25 mile a spur leads off toward the creek at the Big Rock Picnic Area. This spur leads you down to the streamside near the sediment pond. Children love to explore along here in hopes of catching sight of a frog or turtle. After a stop here you can either return to the paved trail or walk up the stream around the sediment pond toward the Kiwanis Building and south play area. It is along the paved trail near the building that the fault movement is most evident.

After observing the evidence you can discuss with the children what

Lake Temescal has wide lawns as well as rugged lakeshore trails.

it means to stand on top of a major earthquake zone, and why the freeway interchange at the northeast end of the park may not have been such a good idea.

Continue around the lake by crossing the footbridge, and there are two trails available. The one to the immediate left follows along the west shore of the lake, and gives the children an opportunity to wade in the shallow waters as they search for water creatures. The one straight ahead climbs the hillside and gives you a chance to view the whole lake with all its waterfowl.

Take either, or both, of these trails, since they are each less than 0.5 mile as they lead back to the parking area.

78. Round Top Trail Loop

Type: Dayhike
Difficulty: Moderate for children
Distance: 2-mile loop
Hiking time: 2 hours
Elevation gain: 450 feet
Hikable: Year-round
Map: East Bay Regional Park District

Sibley Volcanic Regional Preserve was one of the first three parks in the East Bay Regional Park District, along with Lake Temescal and Tilden, and was dedicated in 1936. The 1,763-foot-high Round Top Peak

216

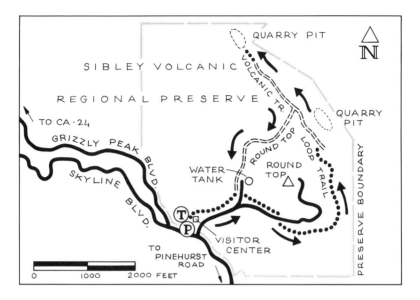

dominates this 386-acre preserve. It now stands as a small, rounded hill among the higher peaks of the Oakland Hills, but it once was the most prominent volcano in what is now the East Bay. This volcano erupted beneath a large freshwater lake about 10 million years ago, and geologists have counted eleven separate lava flows and two violent explosions in the long history of Round Top. Because of this extensive, violent history, Round Top has long been a favorite hike for geologists, amateur and professional, as the quarries operated by the Kaiser Sand and Gravel Company for years exposed volcanic vents and other features.

Take the Fish Ranch Road exit off CA-24 just east of the Caldecott Tunnel. At 0.8 mile take a left off Fish Ranch Road onto Grizzly Peak Boulevard and go for 2.5 miles to the intersection of Grizzly Peak Boulevard and Skyline Boulevard. Make another left turn, and go to the entrance of the preserve.

Pick up the self-guided trail brochure at the visitor center before you begin this hike, so that you don't miss any of the geological features of the preserve. From the center take the trail to the right as it follows the paved road toward the large water tank. At just over 0.25 mile the trail crosses the Round Top Trail Loop and the paved road that leads to the water tank.

The first stop on the self-guided tour is at the tank, so take the short side trip to the left up the paved road, and then return to the trail. Take a left and continue on the trail as it parallels the road, and then crosses it just past 0.5 mile.

The trail now leads around the lower slopes of Round Top through

Open trails are inviting to hikers who like to stretch out as they head toward their goal.

a mixed forest of bay, toyon, Monterey pine, and eucalyptus that is interrupted by occasional open meadows that are brilliant palettes of wildflowers in the spring.

Just past 0.75 mile the view opens up and you can see Mount Diablo to the east, and a large, old quarry pit that exposed the interior of Round Top, an old volcano, as it was dug.

As you pass the old quarry pit, the trail leads through an area of exposed volcanic material and passes the junction of the Volcanic and Round Top trails at about 1 mile. Go straight ahead on the Volcanic Trail until a spur leads off to the right toward the second quarry pit at about 1.25 miles.

The sides of this quarry show large exposed lava flows and an accumulation of red-baked cinders that indicate there was once a volcanic vent there.

Return to the trail junction and take a right on the Round Top Trail Loop to head back to the parking area.

79. Pack Rat Trail Loop

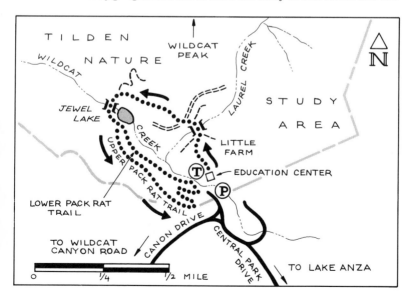

Type: Dayhike
Difficulty: Easy for children
Distance: 1-mile loop
Hiking time: 1 hour
Elevation gain: 100 feet
Hikable: Year-round
Map: East Bay Regional Park District

Little Farm, Jewel Lake, and a free-form environmental education center with displays on various aspects of the East Bay's natural history are all found at the nature study area of Tilden Regional Park. Ohlone Indians lived where the study area is now located, but their population declined rapidly after the invasion of the Spanish. After Europeans settled in the East Bay, much of the area now covered by Tilden Regional Park was used for grazing, particularly the slopes of Wildcat Canyon. In the 1930s a Civilian Conservation Corps camp was built in the canyon, and they planted many trees in the grasslands to protect the watershed. After World War II the Oakland Public Schools and other organizations used the area as a nature school/camp. The park district established a full-time nature study program in the area in the early 1960s. There are 740

Boardwalk leads into a tree-shaded swamp.

acres in the nature study area, with 10 miles of trails, a lake, several ponds, and creeks.

Take Wildcat Canyon Road off Grizzly Peak Boulevard. Turn left on Cañon Drive immediately and follow it to the parking lot for Little Farm.

This short hike begins at Little Farm and the education center. At Little Farm the children will like to play for a while with the collection of animals that changes with the seasons. Sometimes there are donkeys and pigs; at other times, goats, sheep, and calves. After this playtime, head for the education center, where the children can browse through the displays and learn about the trails.

From the center take the Jewel Lake Trail as it leads up a gentle climb and then crosses Laurel Creek at about 0.25 mile and passes Loop Road in another 100 yards. Between Loop Road and Jewel Lake the trail follows in an almost straight line through a shaded forest.

At about 0.5 mile the trail dead ends into the Upper Pack Rat Trail just above Jewel Lake. Take a left on Upper Pack Rat Trail and cross Loop Road after about 100 feet. As you cross the road the trail becomes an elevated boardwalk that crosses a frog-filled marsh that is a fascinating wilderness for young and old alike.

Take a lunch break at the lake and let the children explore around the edges of the marsh as they look for frogs, turtles, small birds, and flying insects.

After the break you can choose between Upper Pat Rat Trail and Lower Pack Rat Trail for your return to the parking area. Lower Pack Rat Trail follows along Wildcat Creek, and offers plenty of opportunity to explore the creekbanks, but is often impassable during wet weather.

If Lower Pack Rat Trail is impassable, take the Upper Pack Rat Trail as it leads along the hillside above the creek and through a forest canopy of evergreen broadleaf trees such as bay and tanoak.

Pay attention to large trees for small items such as these cypress cones.

80. Regional Parks Botanic Garden

Type:	Dayhike
Difficulty:	Easy for children
Distance:	0.5- to 1-mile loop
Hiking time:	1 to 2 hours
Elevation gain:	Minimal
Hikable:	Year-round
Map:	East Bay Regional Park District

The botanic garden was formed in 1940, and is devoted to the collection, growing, display, and preservation of native plants of California. Tilden Regional Park has landscaped a single 10-acre garden so that plants from ten sections and three subsections of California that form 160,000 square miles are all represented. Nearly all the conifers and oaks

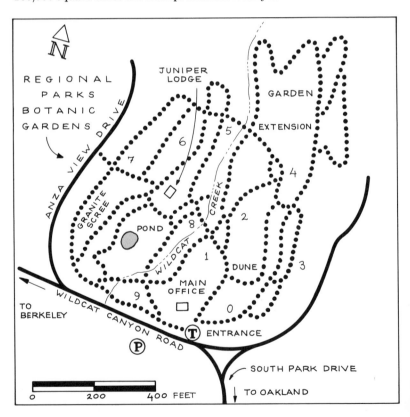

The Native Plant Garden devotes sections to various California plant communities.

found in the state are in the garden, and probably the most complete collection of manzanitas and ceanothuses found anywhere is there. The garden is also expanding its collection of bunchgrasses and aquatic plants. The first plants begin to bloom in the garden in mid-December to January, and continue uninterrupted for the next seven months.

Follow Wildcat Canyon Road into Tilden Regional Park, and the garden is located at the corner of Wildcat Canyon Road and South Park Drive.

There is no set pattern for you to follow along the trails in this small park, but try to visit each of the nine sections that represent different plant communities found in California. You can purchase either *The Guide to the Botanic Garden* or *The Four Seasons, Journal of the Regional Parks Botanic Garden* at the visitor center to help you find all the sections.

81. Seaview/Big Springs Trails Loop

Type: Dayhike
Difficulty: Moderate for children
Distance: 3-mile loop
Hiking time: 2 hours
Elevation gain: 500 feet
Hikable: Year-round
Map: East Bay Regional Park District

Tilden Regional Park adjoins Wildcat Canyon Regional Park, but the two could hardly be more dissimilar in development. There are miles of

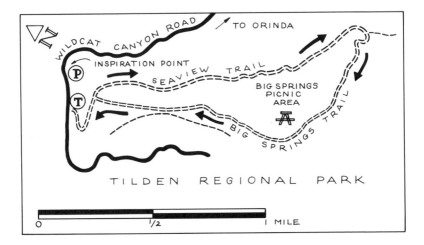

paved roads within Tilden, and several highly developed areas with a golf course, artificial Lake Anza, manicured lawns, a botanic garden, and thousands of people. It is hard to get away from the presence of humans here, but most—luckily for those who seek solitude—stay on the canyon floor. Miles of hiking trails crisscross the hills above the developed areas, however, and there hikers can follow almost impenetrable willow growth along creeks, hike under a thick canopy formed by the oak and bay forests on the slopes above the creeks, and stroll through forests formed by exotic trees such as Monterey pine and eucalyptus. All of these are home to a wide variety of wildlife, particularly birds. Wide meadows of open grassland are interspersed with the forests, and offer brilliant wildflower displays during the spring.

Take Wildcat Canyon Road through Tilden Regional Park 1 mile past the botanic garden, to Inspiration Point. Park in the lot at Inspiration Point and walk back 0.25 mile to the gate marked "Dog Run."

The fire road climbs several switchbacks as it heads through a eucalyptus grove toward the ridge. At about 0.25 mile the trail forks; take the Seaview Trail on the left. It leaves the eucalyptus, and then goes through several small groves of pine. While walking along this stretch you may have the children explore beneath the eucalyptus trees to see how much fallen debris collects there, and then look at the duff of pine needles beneath the pine trees. Both are fire hazards during the hot summer months, but it is easy to see that much more material gathers beneath the eucalyptus trees.

Both the pine and the eucalyptus are exotic species that are not native to the Berkeley Hills. When the first Europeans came to the San Francisco Bay region, the hills were primarily open grasslands with stands of oak and bay, with willows along the creeks. This was also an artificial state, for the Native Americans periodically burned the hills to rid them of the native chaparral to make it easier to hunt deer and to promote the growth of the oak, which provided them with acorns.

By 0.5 mile the trail reaches the high point of the ridge, from which there are panoramic views of the San Francisco Bay and the Contra Costa hills.

For the next 1 mile you walk along a relatively level section of trail with open views to both sides. Have the children pick out familiar landmarks as you hike along, including their own neighborhood if it is visible from the ridge.

At about 1.75 miles the Big Springs Trail leads off to the right, and makes a sharp turn as it begins to head back toward Inspiration Point. The trail drops down into a canyon as it heads toward the Big Springs Picnic Area at 2.25 miles.

This is a good stopping point for lunch where the children can explore around the forest floor for small insects and crawling animals that can be found in dead and decaying limbs and logs.

After the break, stay to the right on the Big Springs Trail as the Quarry Trail leads off to the left. The trail begins to climb back to the level of the Seaview Trail through a mixed forest of oak, bay, pine, and eucalyptus.

At just past 2.75 miles the Big Springs Trail dead ends into the Seaview Trail. Take a left to head back to the parking lot.

The Seaview Trail also offers vistas to the east toward Contra Costa County.

82. Point Isabel Nature Trail

Type: Dayhike
Difficulty: Easy for children
Distance: 1-mile loop
Hiking time: 1 hour
Elevation gain: Level
Hikable: Year-round
Map: East Bay Regional Park District

Small, 21-acre Point Isabel Regional Shoreline park offers excellent views of the Golden Gate and Marin County from the west end of Central Avenue in Richmond just north of Golden Gate Fields. No longer are there the large, spreading buckeyes that grew on the point when the region was first settled. Instead there are large warehouses, including the gigantic blue-and-white U.S.P.S. Bulk Mail Center, where people once picnicked in the shade of the buckeye and looked out toward the Golden Gate. The regional shoreline is small, only about 300 feet wide, and forms an L along the end of the peninsula. Dedicated birdwatchers enjoy the shoreline for its unobstructed views of the mud flats and open water

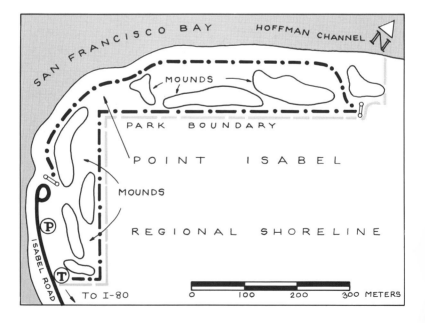

Point Isabel Park offers a chance to stretch your legs and watch sea birds.

where thousands of shorebirds and waterfowl congregate during migration seasons.

Take the Central Avenue exit off I-80 and follow it west to the entrance to Point Isabel.

Begin this hike by heading to the right out of the parking area to the paved path at the beginning of the park. The first 0.5 mile of the trail takes you inland behind the series of small mounds that sometimes block your view of the bay, but it loosens you up as you stride out.

At about 0.5 mile the paved trail comes to a gate, and takes a sharp left. Turn left here and head toward the open water and mud flats. This is the interesting part of the hike as the many shorebirds and water birds become very much the focus of the hike. During the fall migration and spring breeding seasons, this park is one of the best birdwatching spots along the bay. Bring your binoculars and field guides as you take a leisurely stroll back along the last 0.5 mile of the hike to the parking area.

Have the children try to group the birds and see how many of each group they can spot.

After the hike you can picnic on one of the mounds as you continue your watch for different birds.

83. Leeward/Windward Trails Loop

Type: Dayhike
Difficulty: Easy for children
Distance: 2-mile loop
Hiking time: 2 hours
Elevation gain: Minimal
Hikable: Year-round
Map: East Bay Regional Park District

There are about 3 miles of good walking trails on 75-acre Brooks Island. Although the island is only 0.5 mile from the Richmond Marina, it is relatively unknown, and few people get to climb its 160-foot peak. The mud flats surrounding the island make it inaccessible during low tide, and it has become a bird sanctuary with more than 100 species that are known to visit the island and at least 18, including caspian terns and Canada geese, nest there. There are few other animals on the island, but

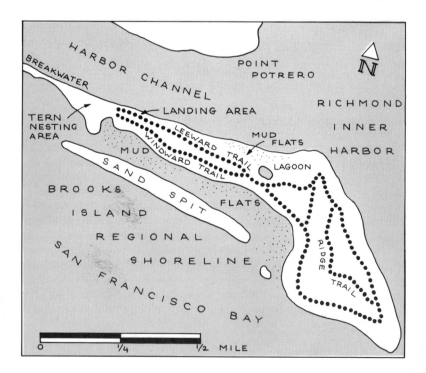

Brooks Island Regional Seashore sits offshore from Point Isabel.

there are two habitats that have almost disappeared from the bay. These are the salt marsh and the coastal strand. Both are easily degraded by pedestrians, and have been protected by the Brooks Island Regional Shoreline preserve. Rare native California bunchgrasses are found inland.

Guided tours of the island area available by reservation for groups (maximum of twenty-five people). Call the park district at 415-636-1684 at least one month in advance of your visit. All visitors must supply their own boat transportation.

All hikes on this island are guided hikes by the parks department, but they generally cover all the trails on the island, and include all natural features.

84. West Ridge/Crest Trails Loop

Type: Dayhike
Difficulty: Moderate for children
Distance: 2-mile loop
Hiking time: 1 hour
Elevation gain: 250 feet
Hikable: Year-round
Map: East Bay Regional Park District

Miller/Knox Regional Shoreline sits among the oil refineries of Richmond and covers 260 acres of Point Richmond. It is more like four separate parks than one, for each of the four sections has its own distinct char-

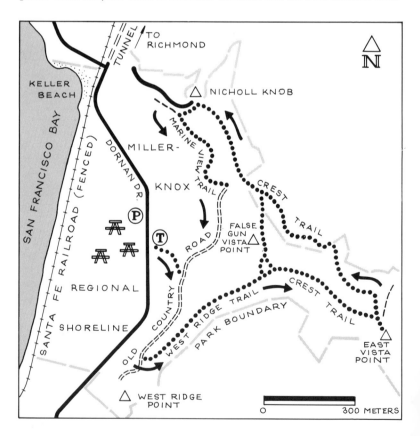

acter, and is used by very different people. Keller Beach is a small beach set in a protected cove where children can play in the sand and water while the adults snooze on shore. A wall of riprap stretches south from the beach, and many people sit on top of the rocks while fishing for flounder or perch, while others simply sit and look across the bay at Marin County. The third area is the 25-acre section of landscaped turf that surrounds a small lagoon. Picnic tables and stunted pine trees are separated from the shoreline by a fence. The fourth area of the shoreline is the upland area where Potrero Hills and Nicholl Knob rise up to overlook the park below. Each of these areas attracts its own followers, and hikers have the upland area almost to themselves.

Take the West Cutting Boulevard exit off I-580 in Richmond. Turn left on West Cutting and go to Garrard Boulevard. Take another left and drive through the tunnel (it becomes Dornan Drive after the tunnel) to the park entrance.

From the parking lot, cross Dornan Drive to the trail that heads toward False Gun Vista Point. At 0.1 mile take a right on the Old Country Road as it winds around the contour of the hills. At 0.3 mile the West Ridge Trail leads off to the left, and about 200 yards farther along is West Ridge Point. You may want to continue to it and make the ascent to the top as you get your children to climb every high point along this route.

After climbing West Ridge Point, return to the junction with the West Ridge Trail and turn right. The trail follows the contours until about 0.75 mile, where the West Ridge Trail leads off to the left to False Gun Vista Point. Take this fork for about 100 yards to the point and climb it before returning to the West Ridge Trail. Return to the junction and take a left on the Crest Trail as it leads to the East Vista Point at about 1 mile.

As you return from the East Vista Point, take the Crest Trail as it heads straight toward Nicholl Knob on the north edge of the park. You reach Nicholl Knob at about 1.75 miles.

Hikers can relax at picnic areas after hiking among the hills of Miller/Knox Regional Shoreline.

Go to your right on the paved road as you leave the knob, and the Marine View Trail leads off to the left after about 100 yards. Turn here and continue back along the Old Country Road to the spur trail that leads back to the parking lot.

If the day is warm you may want to head for Keller Beach, or you may just have a lunch at one of the picnic areas by the parking lot and watch the birds as they flit about near the beach.

85. Bay View/Marsh/Point Trails Loop

Type:	Dayhike
Difficulty:	Moderate for children
Distance:	3-mile loop
Hiking time:	2 hours
Elevation gain:	Level
Hikable:	Year-round
Map:	East Bay Regional Park District

Salt marshes, grasslands, and eucalyptus woodlands are all found in 2,147-acre Point Pinole Regional Shoreline park. While fishing off the concrete pier that extends almost 0.25 mile into the bay is one of the

Small, isolated beaches can be found along the shores of Point Pinole Regional Shoreline.

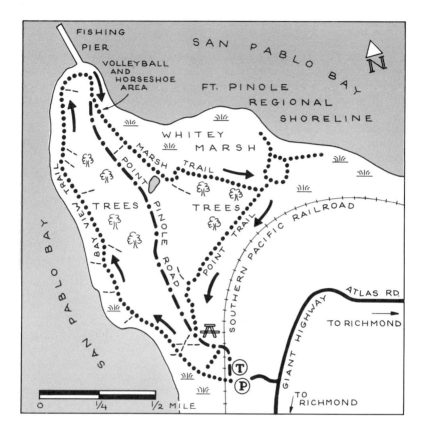

favorite activities of park visitors, birdwatching and hiking are a close second. The square mile of the shoreline is on the Pacific Flyway, and thousands of migrating waterfowl and shorebirds can often be seen there. The wide variety of habitats offers homes to the salt-marsh song sparrow and salt-marsh harvest mouse, native California bunchgrasses such as *Stipa pulchra*, spring wildflowers, and woodland birds not normally found so close to the shore.

Take the Hilltop Drive exit off I-80. Go west to San Pablo Avenue and turn north. From San Pablo turn west on Atlas Road, then south on Giant Highway. On Giant go 0.25 mile to the park entrance.

From the parking area, take the trail to the left that leads toward San Pablo Bay. This is the Bay View Trail and it follows the shoreline for 1 mile to the fishing pier at Pinole Point. About every 200 yards there are short spur trails that lead down to the shoreline, and the children love to take these to see what they can find along the water's edge.

Along this stretch of trail you can watch for shorebirds and water birds that are very numerous here, especially during the fall migration and spring breeding times. The trail passes through a grove of trees at about 0.5 mile.

At the fishing pier you can fish at what has been called the best deep-water fishing spot on the bay, or you can simply sit and watch the birds while you take a break or eat lunch.

After taking a break at the pier, take the Marsh Trail as it leads to the left toward Whittell Marsh. The trail leads past the volleyball and horseshoe areas until it reaches a grove of trees at about 1.5 miles. The Marsh Trail takes off to the left at this fork; the marsh is on the left side of the trail and a grove of trees on the right.

Continue on the trail as it curves around the edge of the marsh and finally ends near the shore. The children will like to explore along the trail in the marsh to see what small animals they can spot in the muck and mud.

Return on the Marsh Trail past the first junction, and take a right at the second. Almost immediately the Marsh Trail leads off to the right and the Point Trail leads straight ahead. Follow the Point Trail through the trees and along the railroad track back to the parking area.

Index

BILL McMILLON has been exploring the outdoors since his boyhood days in Mississippi. A teacher, counselor, and administrator in California and Arizona for seventeen years, Bill now writes full time, and is the author of *Best Hikes With Children: San Francisco's North Bay* (The Mountaineers), *California's Underwater State Parks—A Diver's Guide,* *Volunteer Vacations,* and *Nature Nearby,* among others. He credits his ten-year-old son KEVIN, an enthusiastic hiking companion, as co-author of this book.

Other books you may enjoy from The Mountaineers:

Best Hikes With Children: San Francisco's North Bay, McMillon.
Guide to 90 day hikes in the North Bay area. Includes trail directions
and details, safety, flora and fauna, hiking with kids, and more. Maps
and photos.

**Best Short Hikes in California's Northern Sierra: A Guide to Day
Hikes Near Campgrounds,** Whitehill.
Details on 74 hikes around between the San Joaquin/Mammoth area and
Donner Pass. Includes information on campgrounds and their facilities,
hike distance, difficulty, starting and high points, maps, and photos.

**Best Short Hikes in California's Southern Sierra: A Guide to Day
Hikes Near Campgrounds,** Whitehill.
Features 64 hikes south of Yosemite National Park to the Mineral King
District of Sequoia National Park. Includes information on campgrounds
and their facilities, hike distance, difficulty, starting and high points,
maps, and photos.

Best Short Hikes In and Around the North Sacramento Valley, Soares.
75 day hikes within an hour's drive of the Valley. Includes Castle Crags,
Shasta Lake, Whiskeytown Lake, McArthur-Burney Falls, Hat Creek and
Pit River, Yolla Bollys and Coast Range, Redding, Anderson, Red Bluff,
Chico, and Oroville.

Hiking the Southwest's Canyon Country, Hinchman.
Six two-to three-week itineraries of dayhikes, backpacks and scenic drives
in Colorado, Utah, New Mexico, and Arizona. Includes distance, duration,
topographical maps, difficulty, and more.

Best Hikes With Children in Western and Central Oregon, Henderson.
100 easily-accessible hikes, many lesser-known, with detailed trail information. Tips on hiking with kids, safety, and wilderness ethics.

Day Hikes From Oregon's Campgrounds, Ostertag.
Guide to campgrounds that access the best hikes and nature walks in
Oregon. Facilities, hike descriptions, more.

**Exploring Oregon's Wild Areas: A Guide for Hikers, Backpackers,
X-C Skiers & Paddlers,** Sullivan. Detail-stuffed guidebook to Oregon's
65 wilderness areas, wildlife refuges, nature preserves, and state parks.

Available from your local bookstore or outdoor store, or from The Mountaineers Books, 1011 SW Klickitat Way, Suite 107, Seattle, WA 98134.
Or call for a catalog of over 200 outdoor books: 1-800-553-4453.

The MOUNTAINEERS, founded in 1906, is a non-profit outdoor activity and conservation club, whose mission is "to explore, study, preserve and enjoy the natural beauty of the outdoors . . . ." Based in Seattle, Washington, the club is now the third largest such organization in the United States, with 12,000 members and four branches throughout Washington State.

The Mountaineers sponsors both classes and year-round outdoor activities in the Pacific Northwest, which include hiking, mountain climbing, ski-touring, snowshoeing, bicycling, camping, kayaking and canoeing, nature study, sailing, and adventure travel. The club's conservation division supports environmental causes through educational activities, sponsoring legislation, and presenting informational programs. All club activities are led by skilled, experienced volunteers, who are dedicated to promoting safe and responsible enjoyment and preservation of the outdoors.

The Mountaineers Books, an active, non-profit publishing program of the club, produces guidebooks, instructional texts, historical works, natural history guides, and works on environmental conservation. All books produced by The Mountaineers are aimed at fulfilling the club's mission.

If you would like to participate in these organized outdoor activities or the club's programs, consider a membership in The Mountaineers. For information and an application, write or call The Mountaineers, Club Headquarters, 300 Third Avenue West, Seattle, Washington 98119; (206) 284-6310.

Send or call for our catalog of over 200 outdoor books:
The Mountaineers Books
1011 SW Klickitat Way, Suite 107
Seattle, WA 98134
1-800-553-4453